Modern Swimming and Training Techniques

Modern Swimming and Training Techniques

For Coach and Competitor

Roger Eady

Arthur Barker Limited
5 Winsley Street London W1

ISBN 0 213 99418 6

Printed in Great Britain by Bristol Typesetting Co Ltd
Barton Manor Bristol

Contents

Preface

Every month I learn something new in the field of competitive swimming coaching, so it would be impossible for me to write an 'encyclopaedia' of training. It is my intention to let the reader look at the sport through my eyes and draw his own conclusions. I cannot be dogmatic because coaching, like any healthy business, cannot afford to stand still. It must be always changing and searching for more efficient methods of obtaining the best results. Once a coach or swimmer becomes satisfied, his career is finished.

Training is still very much an art but each year the scientist adds more information to the physiology and psychology of conditioning. Better equipped people than myself have already covered these aspects adequately and for that reason the book will not be too technical.

Competition in society and swimming is becoming more intense and body and mind are placed under ever-increasing stress. To prepare swimmers for the stresses they will find in competition we must give them ample experience in training. The art of coaching is to know how much mental and physical stress can be placed upon the individual without destroying his interest in the sport.

I hope that after reading this book coach and swimmer will be encouraged to take a deeper interest in their training to offset the inevitable boredom of an ill-conceived programme because neither of them can afford to become blasé; after all it was Socrates who said, ' If I am wise, it is only because I know I am ignorant.'

1 Mechanics of Swimming

Without a clear understanding of the most efficient method of propelling the body through the water swimmers and coaches will be severely handicapped in their struggle for better performance. If they are armed with a sound theoretical background of mechanics, the rules governing the four competitive strokes can be exploited to the full. Just because a world record-holder swims a stroke in a particular fashion this does not mean that every 'budding champion' should copy him. There are no two people who are built exactly alike: we all vary in body shape, size, length of arms and legs, size of feet, strength and flexibility of joints. For these reasons it is impossible to stereotype swimmers or any other person. Even a mass-produced car can perform differently from its identical brothers. We accept that we are all different and that the coach's job is to examine the individual and develop a method of moving through the water that is both efficient and within the swimmer's physical capabilities. In this chapter many of these problems of propulsion will be considered.

Flotation

There are people in the world who cannot stay on or near to the surface of the water when attempting to swim, but competitive swimmers will never be faced with this problem. The only two components in the human body that float (have a specific gravity (SG) less than one) are the fat on our body and the air contained in our lungs. Without them human beings would never be able to move through the water, because any part of the body with a specific gravity greater than one would sink. Teeth (SG 2.24), hair (SG 1.3) and skin (SG 1.1), not to mention bones and muscles, are all components that do not float. In the majority of human beings fat (SG 0.942) and air offset the other parts of the body and help it stay afloat. Individuals with tremendous lung capacities and layers of fat on their bodies should find floating a simple task (figure 1). Their counterparts with little fat and small lungs may struggle to stay near the surface of the water unless they have small bones and muscles. Yet though the fat person may find it very easy to float in the water, it will be shown later on in this chapter that the rotund shape can also be a disadvantage.

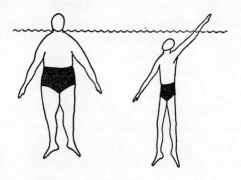

Figure 1

How the body floats in water is also important and the distribution of fat and air in the body will affect the position dramatically. The majority of young males have very little fat in their body, so they have to rely heavily on the air in their lungs to keep them afloat. A male who attemps to lie in the prone position in the water (figure 2) will soon find his lower body sinking because there is very little fat and no air in his

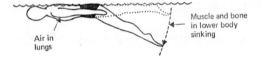

Figure 2

legs and pelvis to keep the bones and muscles afloat. The air in the lungs will support the chest and upper body and keep it on or near the surface of the water.

Once the female reaches puberty she generally accumulates layers of fat round the thighs and hips which helps to support the weight of the muscle and bones in the legs (figure 3). She has smaller bones and muscles than the average man and thus her fat and air make her a great deal more buoyant than a man.

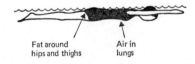

Figure 3

It should be understood that there are very few people who can maintain a prone position in the water without their legs sinking, but that because of their additional layers of fat, women's legs are slower to sink than the male's.

Once a body is floating it is weightless and therefore its mass and shape is going to dictate how efficiently it can be moved through the water.

Streamlining and Resistance

Every person has a size and a shape which causes resistance as it moves through the water. The bigger and more irregular the shape the greater resistance or drag it causes as it moves through the water. Builders of any racing yacht or powerboat realize that to construct a hull which allows water to flow freely round will increase its chances of moving unimpeded by drag. Figure 4a illustrates the perfect shape for a body in water: that of an aircraft wing.

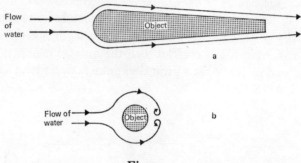

Figure 4

A round object, as in figure 4b does not allow a free flow of water past it but hampers and causes changes in the direction of the current. The fat person who finds it very easy to float has considerable difficulty in moving through the water because his shape corresponds to that illustrated in figure 4b. The perfect swimmer would have a body shape as illustrated in figure 4a; there is no such individual, but many sprint swimmers have a body shape which has many characteristics of figure 4a. Roland Mathes, the East German world record-holder over 100 metres and 200 metres backcrawl, typifies the body shape of a sprinter (figure 5). He is over six feet tall with broad

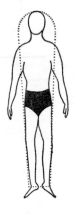

Figure 5   Figure 6

shoulders, narrow hips and long, slim, tapering legs. He complies most favourably with 'the perfect shape' except for the lack of a 'dome-shaped' head to start the smooth flow of water past him. I don't consider it to be pure coincidence that Mathes and many other world-class sprinters are tall and slim with a steady taper of the body from the shoulders down to the hips.

As we have seen, widening of the hips is a characteristic of puberty in women; although they may have long slim legs and slim shoulders, this 'midriff bulge' can disrupt the smooth flow of water round the body and set up a considerable resistance (figure 6). This is one of the many reasons why women are not as fast as men: their bodies create greater resistance. Nobody should run away with the idea that unless a person is tall and lean and shaped like an aircraft wing he is unlikely to become a world-class swimmer, because there are many exceptions to this rule. A streamlined body is a help to a swimmer, but there are many other components to be considered. Nikolia Pankin, the Russian breaststroker and ex-world record holder over 100 metres and 200 metres, is short and stocky, thus proving that it would be very wrong of coaches to exclude swimmers from training because they do not adhere to a certain body type.

Whatever the shape of his body, the swimmer can do a great deal in the water to cut down its resistance. The human body floats *in* and not on the water, as illustrated in figure 1. The amount of fat and air in our body will determine the final position in the water. For ease of movement the ideal position for the body to float, either prone or supine, is parallel to the surface (figure 7a). If the body is allowed to move into a

Figure 7

position at an angle (figure 7b) to the surface of the water, when the swimmer attempts to move forward the water will resist the movement of the body and thus impede its progress. Coaches and swimmers throughout the world are constantly working to cut down the resistance of the body in the water and whatever their shape or size swimmers can always improve this position.

The important lesson to be learnt from this chapter so far is that unnecessary resistance of the body in water is a hindrance.

Propulsion

There is no point in a swimmer's having a perfectly shaped body causing little resistance if he does not have an efficient way of propelling it through the water. Man moves round on land by using his legs, and occasionally his arms, to lever his body in different directions. The speed and direction of the movement is determined by the application of Newton's third law of motion: 'To every action there is an equal and opposite reaction'. In other words, if we exert a pressure of twenty pounds with our hands against a wall, the wall will react by sending back a pressure of twenty pounds against the hand

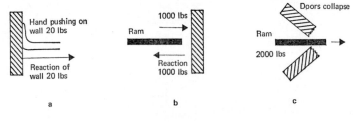

Figure 8

(figure 8a). It was common practice in medieval times for armies laying siege to castles to batter the doors down with huge logs. Many soldiers were employed to lift and propel the battering ram against the doors. Imagine the missile hitting the doors with a pressure of one thousand pounds (figure 8b) and bouncing off. The doors have produced a one-thousand-pound reaction to the ram and sent it hurtling back in the direction it came from. If a bigger ram is used with a pressure of two thousand pounds the doors may not be strong enough (figure 8c) to send back a two-thousand-pound reaction and they thus collapse under the strain. The law of action and re-action applies when the buffers at a terminal railway station bring a train to rest: the buffers provide reaction in the op-posite direction to force exerted on it by the train. It follows that whatever direction a swimmer wishes to move in the water he must apply force in the opposite direction. Imagine a swimmer lying in the prone position in the water (figure 9a);

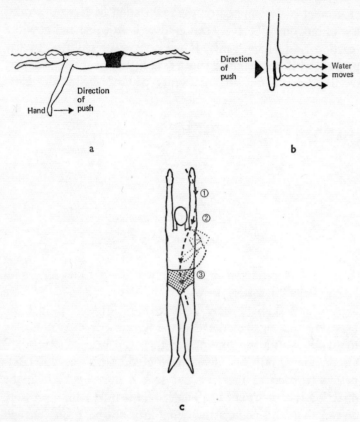

Figure 9

when he wishes to move forward he applies pressure with his hands on the water in the opposite direction to his proposed course. Water is not solid like a wooden door or a piece of metal, so that when the hand applies great pressure in a par-

Stanley gasped, his blushes forgotten. If Demolition Dan wasn't *very* careful he was going to damage his shiny new yellow bulldozer by knocking into the trees of Bluebell Wood!

As he watched, the bulldozer lurched forward and biffed a tree.

A squirrel fell out and landed on the head of Stanley's dad, Herbert, where it sat like a wig with feet, wondering where its nest had suddenly gone to.

Stanley took out his cocoa tin, selected a piece of secret tripe, and popped it into his mouth.

FLASH!

Plain, timid Stanley Gawthorpe disappeared, and in his place stood...

ACCRINGTON STANLEY!
-Hero of the People!

The old folk cheered.

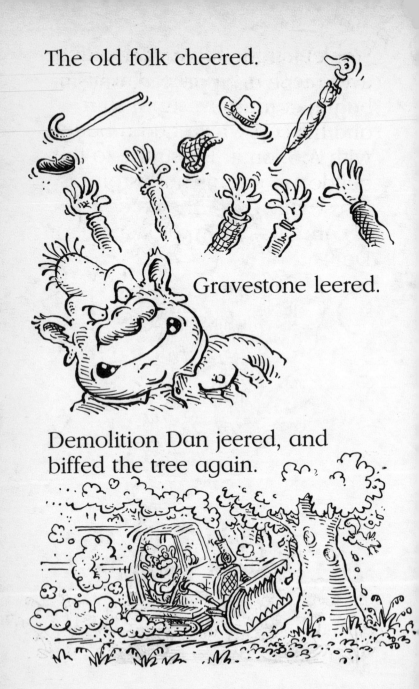

Gravestone leered.

Demolition Dan jeered, and
biffed the tree again.

Stanley strode forward, looking every inch a superhero in his baggy corduroys, stripy shirt and his cap which had a badge with **A.S.** on it. He strode to the bulldozer, put his hands on his hips (which superheros do a lot of) and looked up at Demolition Dan.

"I am Accrington Stanley," he said in his most manly voice, "and I right all wrongs, correct all mistakes, and give 'elp where it is most needed."

"Buzz off!" snarled Dan, and gave the tree another biff.

This time, the squirrel's nest fell out of the tree, and jammed itself firmly over Dan's head.

Try as he would, Dan could not pull it off, partly because a couple of the twigs in the nest had jammed themselves up his piggy nostrils.

At the same time, Dan's foot jammed itself hard down on the accelerator.

49

Stanley was most concerned for
the bulldozer *and* the tree,
which were jammed up against
each other.

Using all his Accrington Stanley
strength, he lifted the bulldozer,
turned it round, pointed it in the
direction of the main road, and
set it back down again.

There were two things that Stanley hadn't noticed:

1) There was a pond between him and the main road

and

2) Gravestone Grimshaw was between him and the pond.

Because the accelerator was jammed, the bulldozer's wheels were spinning fast, so that when Stanley set it down, it shot off like a rocket.

Gravestone saw the bulldozer heading straight for him, and decided that this was, quite definitely, *not* the place to be.

His face turned the colour of vanilla ice cream, then he screeched "Yaaaaark!" turned round and ran.

As he ran, he was looking over his shoulder, which was why he didn't see the pond until the water was up to his fat tum, but still he kept running, his legs threshing round like a windmill.

Before Stanley could save him
(which, as a true superhero,
was Stanley's first instinct) the
bulldozer, with Demolition
Dan, plunged in. It was as
Stanley suspected – the
bulldozer couldn't swim.

It sank straight to the bottom, until only its exhaust pipe was sticking out above the water, blowing little smoke rings which looked, to Fleabag, like doughnuts with a hole in the middle.

It wasn't until he jumped up and chewed one that he decided he'd been wrong.

Stanley could feel the effects of the secret tripe wearing off, and then suddenly...PLOP...they did wear off, and he was plain, timid, Stanley Gawthorpe again.

No one saw him change back because everybody was watching the pond.

Two little pointy heads had bobbed up by this time, and Stanley watched as Dan and Gravestone Grimshaw hauled themselves from the slimy pond looking like walking mud pies and spitting out tadpoles.

They squelched off into the
distance, the cheers from the
old folk ringing in their
sticky-out ears.

Chapter Six

Next day, after school, Stanley went along to Bluebell Wood.

Everything was exactly as he thought it would be, with the birds singing, the bees humming and the butterflies fluttering by.

Exactly as he thought it would be – except for one thing. The big supermarket sign had gone.

And the old folk were not sitting on their benches eating sandwiches – no, they were sitting round a bonfire, which Stanley thought was rather strange since the weather was quite warm.

"Wonder where they got the wood from?" he thought to himself.

That evening, on the local television news, there was a story of how the supermarket was not, after all, going to build a store in Bluebell Wood.

They also told of how Bluebell Wood had been saved from being knocked down by superhero Accrington Stanley.

Stanley was puzzled – all he had done was show Demolition Dan the right way to the main road, or at least, Accrington Stanley had.

He smiled to himself. He was quite certain that nobody knew that he and Accrington Stanley were the same person.

But then, why did Stanley's dad bake Stanley an extra special tripe pie with dumplings for his tea?

And when he put it on the table, why did he look at Stanley, crinkle up his face, and say "thank you"?

ticular direction (figure 9b), the water in front of the hand begins to move; instead of reacting to the force of the hand it gives, like the castle door, under the pressure. While the hand is pushing backwards it must also move in a zig-zag pattern to search for still water which will react to the pressure of the hands (figure 9c). It is imperative that the paddles can find still water to apply pressure on, because the body moves through the water by using the ' third class of levers '. Figure 10 shows how this class is applied to propulsion in the water. The hand must act as a fulcrum and fix itself in the water; if this is done successfully the body will be propelled past the hand by con-

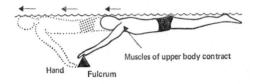

Figure 10

tracting muscles in the arms and upper body. A beginner in swimming may be pushing his hand backwards, but until he clearly understands that his hand is a fulcrum he may never seek still water to fix his hand in. The right ' feeling ' is important to the swimmer; he should sense that his body is being pulled past his hand by the muscles in his upper body.

The size of the paddle used is also very important in propulsion. It would be true to say that swimmers with large hands and feet could find them advantageous. The largest hand paddle is shown in figure 11a: fingers fully extended and slightly apart. If the fingers are left wide open as in 11b the water slips

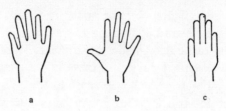

Figure 11

between them and the hand can never 'fix'. For convenience many coaches recommend swimmers to keep their fingers together when pulling in the water (figure 11c), because keeping the fingers slightly apart demands considerable strength in the hands. A common fault in the frontcrawl pull is for a swimmer to fix his hand too deep in the water and find that he has not the strength to lever his body past his hand. He solves the problem by spreading his fingers wide apart and letting his hand slip through the water (figure 12a). If the swimmer shortens the length of his lever by bending his arm and brings his hand nearer to his shoulder he is able to keep his fingers together, fix his hand in the water and lever his body over his hand. By shortening his lever the swimmer finds that his available strength is sufficient to move his body.

The feet are another means of propulsion, especially in breaststroke. Newton's third law of motion is applied by the feet to as much still water as possible. Individual differences in joint flexibility and foot size dictate the amount of propulsion to be gained. In the 'flutter kick' of backcrawl and frontcrawl the toes are extended as much as possible. Figure 13a shows a swimmer with flexible ankle joints. When the toes are fully extended they point towards the bottom of the pool; as they are kicked upwards the water is pushed backwards by the top of the foot. A little forward propulsion is obtained by

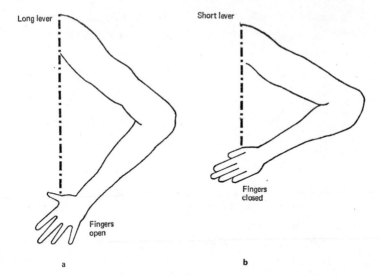

Long lever

Short lever

Fingers open

Fingers closed

a

b

Figure 12

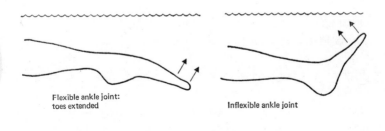

Flexible ankle joint: toes extended

Inflexible ankle joint

a

b

Figure 13

pressing the water backwards. Figure 13b shows a person with inflexible ankles; when his toes are fully extended the top of the foot is not in a position to push the water backwards, but does so upwards. This person would not obtain forward propulsion from his leg kick.

B

In the breaststroke leg kick where the toes are turned outwards (figure 14), the large surface area of the instep applies

Figure 14

pressure on the water by using the powerful muscles of the
upper leg. In still water the reaction is very powerful and the
body is able to lever itself away from the feet, which are fixed
in the water.

All information on resistance and propulsion must be care-
fully studied and applied to the individual swimmer. Because
individuals vary in strength and physique, flexibility and size
of paddles the coach should consider the individual's strong
points and adapt them to the mechanical ideals and the laws
governing a particular stroke. Once this has been done it is the
duty of a totally committed coach to persuade his swimmers
to improve upon any weaknesses they may have. The first
attempt at a particular stroke may bring early success but it
may not be the most efficient means of propulsion from the
point of view of the swimmer's long-term objectives. Compromise is too often the easy way; a swimmer who lacks strength
should be encouraged to become stronger, not to scale down
his stroke to his own level. This may have to be done as a
short-term measure, but coach and swimmer should have the
ultimate 'blueprint' in their heads and work towards it.
Efficient propulsion in the water will be gained by marrying
stroke laws, mechanics and an individual's assets. Nobody can

give a clear answer on how best to do this because, though science can give us the mechanical answers, its application to a human being is the real art of coaching. The coach should always be searching for better ways of presenting his ideas to the swimmers, so that they will stimulate their desire to learn and improve. Before getting too involved in the intricate details of a particular stroke technique the coach should make sure that his swimmers have a clear idea of how best their body moves through the water and the ideal method of propelling it. All of us have different amounts of natural ability, but even the best will take a keener interest in their activity if they understand what they are doing. The ability to learn depends on a person's powers of concentration, which are always stimulated by an interest in the activity pursued. Throughout this book the problem of offering work which is challenging and interesting will frequently recur.

Many activities can be designed to encourage swimmers to take an interest in how they move in the water, depending on age and intelligence. Even the international swimmer can improve his ability to search for and apply force on still water. An inexperienced swimmer can soon grasp a working knowledge of streamlining and the use of his hands as paddles and then transfer this information into improving his strokes.

The following chapters will be devoted to the application of mechanics to the four recognized competitive swimming strokes and their appropriate racing starts and turns. Nothing should be taken for granted and constant reference to this chapter will be made in an attempt to build up a stroke which is based on sound mechanical principles.

2 Butterfly

The baby of the four competitive strokes, butterfly, requires rather more strength and mobility than the others to perform efficiently. The stroke was developed from breaststroke in the early 1950s and was given autonomy in 1953, but there is still a reluctance on the part of many coaches to devote as much time to its development as to the other strokes. In Australia and America it is common for six-year-olds to train on this stroke without showing signs of excessive fatigue, and in fact a great deal of personal satisfaction is derived from being able to train on butterfly. 'Uncle Sam' has all the world's butterfly talent so it would be foolish of any other nation to say they know as much about the stroke as the Americans. The British have not had sufficient experience in developing the stroke among large numbers of people and producing world record holders. There is a whole world of difference between theoretical knowledge and its application to practical problems.

Body Position

The body should be parallel with the surface of the water so as to cut resistance down to an absolute minimum. Also the FINA ruling states that the body must stay in the prone position with the shoulders parallel to the surface. The normal body position is illustrated in figure 15a, where the face is kept in the water, eyes looking forwards along the bottom of the pool. If the head is lifted up too high a reaction occurs in the hips and legs and the bottom half of the body begins to sink (figure 15b). A girl whose legs and hips are very buoyant may find that by holding her head in the normal position the bottom

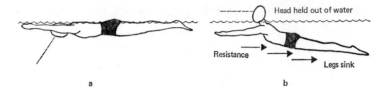

Figure 15

half of her body begins to lift out of the water and she is no longer parallel to the surface. In other words, by juggling about with the position of the head in the water the individual's body position can be altered to suit her needs. It does not need very much experience to note that women have a higher body position in the water than men because of their better fat distribution. It is not possible to make a person float higher in the water but we can streamline his body and cut its resistance down to a minimum.

Leg Kick

The main function of the leg kick is to help maintain a flat body position by keeping the rear end of the swimmer near to the surface. It also stabilizes the body when the arms are entering the water and pulling. The legs keep the body on an even keel while the arms are pulling it along as in a sailing boat where the rudder keeps the boat on the right course and the sails drive the body forward. If the legs were left to trail in the water the majority of swimmers would feel them sinking and causing drag; the body would no longer be a stable platform for the arms to work from but would undulate through the water. This problem will be considered in the timing of the stroke. The kick is performed by the swimmer extending his legs and feet behind him, keeping them close together. The FINA rulings deal with all the competitive swimming strokes and the reader is asked to consult them if he is not certain how a particular stroke or part of a stroke should be performed. From this trailing position both legs move upwards together and the knees begin to bend and move apart (figure 16a). The toes turn inwards and the legs press downwards on the water, which forces the toes backwards (figure 16b). A swimmer with very flexible ankles will be able to push the water backwards with the instep and thus gain some sort of propulsion. When the legs straighten out again they are moved back towards the surface of the water by the swimmer bending his knees slightly and moving his hips upwards. Swimmers should be encouraged to start the leg kick from the hip with very little knee bend and not to kick too deeply, as their legs will cause the body to drag if they sink too deeply. Ideally, a swimmer would perform an efficient leg kick within

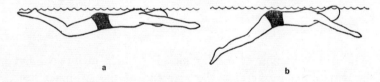

Figure 16

the depth of his body. The power of leg kick will vary with the individual, but as long as the body remains flat without excessive undulation it is doing its job efficiently. The number of leg kicks for each arm cycle will be dealt with in the section on timing.

Arm Action

The arms and hands are the major forms of propulsion in the butterfly stroke. There have been cases of swimmers who are able to perform fifty metres of butterfly leg kick in thirty-two seconds, which is very good indeed. It is true to say that the swimmer would be able to move much faster on his arms only if they were used efficiently, so it is sensible to develop the arm action as the real power-house of the stroke.

So far we have dealt with the streamlining of the body, but this can easily be disrupted by a poor arm action. Flexibility of the shoulder joints is vital to butterfly success; if a swimmer cannot lie flat in the water and recover his arms without disturbing his body he will have little success in this stroke. The more the shoulders have to be lifted out of the water to help the arms in their recovery, the more the flat body position will be disturbed. When the shoulders or head are lifted out of the water the hips and legs move downwards and so begin to drag. Depending on shoulder mobility the arms are thrown forward, together, over the water and the hands enter the water either in front of the shoulders or just outside. Arms are almost fully extended in front of the body as the hands enter the water. Fingers should enter first, with the hand ready to act as a paddle. Some coaches say that entry is not as important as the pull under the surface. There is a certain amount of truth in this statement but I have found that an efficient entry of the hands puts a swimmer into a good pulling position very quickly. As soon as the hands have entered the water they should try to fix themselves so that the arms can lever the body past them. The hands cannot remain in one position throughout the pull because the water soon begins to move, the hand slips and a fulcrum can no longer be maintained. A keyhole type of pull then develops, as shown in figure 17.

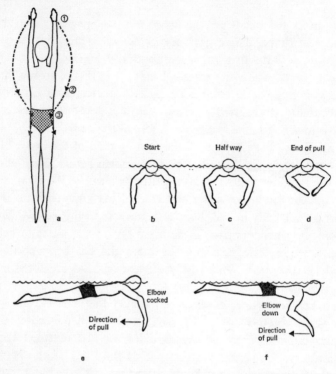

Figure 17

A swimmer with long levers and a great deal of strength will take fewer strokes over fifty metres than his short-levered counterpart, especially if he has the ability to fix his hands in the water. Imagine swimmer X who can place his hands into the water three feet in front of his head and fix them there. If his hands never slipped one single inch (which is impossible), he would take half the strokes of swimmer Y, who can place his hands only one and a half feet in front of his head, to swim a set distance. Once his hands are in the water a swimmer should be conscious of applying pressure to them and not dropping his elbow (figure 17e), because the latter does not allow the hand to push the water backwards. Halfway through the pull the hands come very close together and begin to push backwards on the water rather than pull. When the hands have finished the push they lift out of the water and recover over the surface normally by moving round the sides of the body with the arms straight and the hands relaxed. Throughout the pull the arms trace a keyhole path, but the palms of the hands should always be pushing backwards. The amount of bending of the elbow will depend on the strength and length of levers of the individual. Doug Russell, the 1968 Olympic 100-metre butterfly champion, impressed me with his ability to use his long arms to lever his body through the water; his stroke was slow and deliberate compared to the other swimmers in his race. It was interesting to compare his stroke rate with two Japanese butterfly swimmers who had very short arms and had to stroke much faster to stay anywhere near him. Swimmers should strive to improve their speed by cutting down the amount of hand slip and developing sufficient muscle strength to speed up their arm action. In the case of two swimmers who can lever their bodies equal distances on each arm pull, the winner of the race will be the one who can do it faster. The quality and rate of pull should thus be a major priority in all strokes.

Breathing

The normal body position of butterfly means that the face is immersed in the water. Any movement of the head from this position, however slight, will disturb the body. When deciding on the method of breathing in butterfly the coach has to bear in mind how frequently he is going to allow the body to be disturbed, because there will be an increase in resistance if the head is lifted upwards or turned to the side. A swimmer could breathe at the completion of every arm pull, but that would mean that his body would be in a perfectly streamlined position for only about a half of each stroke. The other extreme would be to hold the breath too long and build up a phenomenal oxygen debt to the muscles. The sensible solution is to adopt a method and pattern of breathing to suit the individual and the distance to be swum. Sprinters often hold their breath for the first six or eight strokes of a race, whereas 200-metre swimmers usually adopt a pattern of breathing every two strokes because they have a long way to go and they want to keep up a constant supply of oxygen to their muscles.

The breathing pattern, then, will depend on these factors. When the arms have completed the first half of the pull and are moving into the pushing stage the head begins to lift or turn to breathe. Lifting the head and breathing to the front is the most common procedure, so that will be dealt with first. Just before the mouth clears the water the excess air is expelled from the lungs by the swimmer blowing out through his nose and mouth, so that a fresh supply of oxygen can be taken in without delay. A sensible coaching point is to insist that the chin remain in the water when the swimmer is breathing to avoid any unnecessary lifting of the head. As soon as the breath is taken in, the face should return into the water to maintain a streamlined body. Once the face is back in the water some individuals begin to breathe out slowly and deliberately until their lungs are empty and they are ready to lift their head and breathe again. This is called 'trickle breathing'. It has been my experience that the majority of swimmers hold their breath through the first half of the pull and only breathe out in one big blast just before their mouth clears the water to take in a new supply of air (explosive breathing). Coaches argue on the merits of both methods; for a two-stroke breathing pattern the explosive method seems to be the better, but I am always prepared to experiment.

Turning the head to the side, as in frontcrawl, is another way of breathing. Glenda Phillips of Wales and Ross Wales of America have achieved great successes using side breathing. The main problem associated with side breathing is that the body begins to slow down during the breathing cycle because the arms have almost finished pulling and consequently sinks down in the water; the head thus has to be turned right round to the side of the body to get a breath of air. This extreme movement of head and neck can cause the body to twist and increase its resistance. I have direct experience of only one swimmer who uses side breathing and I do feel that his fluency of movement would be improved if he were to breathe to the front. Again we come to the question of the art of coaching when we apply these methods to the individual. Ultimate success is the only yardstick by which to measure the methods. Whatever method of breathing is adopted the efficiency of the stroke should not be disturbed.

Timing

It is of little use having an efficient arm action and leg kick if they cannot work together in an efficient manner. When the arms enter the water the reaction at the other end of the body is for the legs to kick down; by halfway through the pull the legs have kicked back up to the surface of the water and are on their way down to perform a second kick. They normally execute two kicks for every one complete arm pull, so as to stop any excessive undulation of the body caused by the powerful arm entry and pull. Unless a swimmer has very buoyant legs one kick would not be enough to stop the back end of the body sinking. As the arms move faster and more powerfully the front half of the body begins to lift in the water and the legs kick harder to keep the back part in line with the chest. In other words, the legs should respond to the work being done by the arms and keep everything finely balanced. The majority of one-beat leg kicks that I have seen are not fulfilling this role efficiently.

To summarize then, the propulsion in butterfly is derived from a powerful and continuous arm pull with no glide and the leg kick keeps the body in a streamlined position.

Butterfly Start

For all starts, the entry into the water should be streamlined and shallow, as this position causes less resistance and there will therefore be a smoother passage through the water (figure 18b). The position that the swimmer takes on the block will dictate the power and direction that his body takes when leaving the block. The objective of the start is to move as far down the pool as possible at, or faster than, normal racing speed without having to expend energy in performing the stroke. Once the body has slowed down to normal racing speed no time should be lost in breaking the surface and starting the stroke. If the dive is smooth and shallow, as in 18b, the swimmer will break the surface as his body reaches normal racing speed.

The starting position on the blocks is shown in figure 18a, with feet comfortably apart and toes gripping the edge. The knees are bent and the body arched forward with the eyes looking down the pool. Balance is maintained by the arms, which are stretched out in front of the body, and the centre of gravity now passes through the balls of the feet. The body is

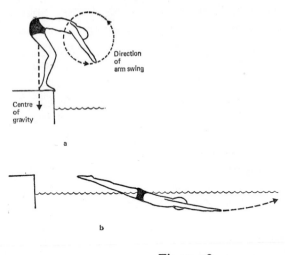

Figure 18

poised and coiled waiting for the 'off', when it will spring to life. On the command 'Go!' the swimmer topples forward and drives his arms backwards, applying force with his feet into the front edge of the block. It is this edge which will send back an equal and opposite force to drive his body forward and outwards from the side of the pool. Some swimmers prefer to perform a 'wind up' start, which means that their arms move in a backwards circle (as in figure 18a). Research suggests that this could be the best way of increasing the power of the drive off the blocks. Every swimmer should experiment with different arm actions in the start and find the best way for him. Once he has left the block he should streamline his body as in figure 18b, making sure that hands and feet are together and toes pointed and entering the water in a shallow dive, with the fingers breaking the surface and the body following through the hole. At one time it was considered necessary for a swimmer to throw his body as far away from the side as possible and 'belly flop' onto the surface. This method causes terrific resistance to the forward motion of the body in the water and a clean shallow entry is far more efficient and less painful.

The same streamlined position used in flight should be maintained under the water to allow the body to move with the minimum of resistance. Just before breaking the surface of the water many swimmers start the dolphin leg kick because they find that this helps to get them into the rhythm of their stroke with the minimum of delay. Tall swimmers should have a great advantage over any others because they can enter the water in a shallow dive farther away from the side. All physical advantages like these should be fully exploited through the development of sound technique. A very tall and leading butterfly swimmer in Wales was persistently dropping his legs when he performed a butterfly start. His feet would touch the surface of the water before his hands and he was setting up considerable resistance as his body ploughed onto the surface rather than entering cleanly through the water. He eventually solved his problem after seeing a video film of himself in action.

Most faults in the start occur in the legs and feet. Once again we are concerned with the ability of the body to stream-line and cut down resistance to forward movement. This problem is also associated with turning.

Butterfly Turns

The sooner a swimmer can get his feet onto the wall the quicker he will be able to push off and continue his race. The 'push-off' is very important but unless the feet can be placed on the wall quickly an efficient push-off will be only partly successful. To comply with the rules of butterfly a swimmer must touch the wall with both hands simultaneously and on the same plane with the body, lying squarely on the breast. As soon as both hands have touched the wall, ideally with the arms at full stretch, the swimmer should take one arm away from the side and bend his knees to help bring his feet up to the wall in the least possible time. Most swimmers prefer to take their left arm away first and drop their shoulder under the water while their feet come through to the wall. Once the feet are firmly on the wall the rest of the body should be under the water with the arms outstretched and a powerful push-off is begun. The body is on its side, but as it pushes off it twists on to its front because, to comply with the rules the body must be breast downwards when the feet leave the wall.

I have stressed the importance of trying to touch the wall with the arms at full stretch; this means that the body can turn well away from the wall and there is plenty of room for the legs to come under the body and perform a powerful push-off. We push off with our legs and feet, so there is no point in bringing the rest of our body too near the wall. A good turn is very much like a ball rebounding off a wall: the faster it hits the wall, the faster it bounces off. The same should apply in swimming turns. Don't slow your body down by holding the wall with your hands but get your feet through quickly and let your legs rebound your body off the wall. When jumping into the air a person never crouches down on the floor first; he bends his knees to only about ninety degrees for maximum thrust. The same appears true of push-offs.

Once the body has left the wall it should streamline itself, as in the start, and as soon as it slows down to normal racing speed the head should break the surface of the water and continue the stroke. The velocity of the body in a start and turn is greater than any swimming speed and coach and swimmer should exploit this advantage to the full.

3 Backcrawl

Modern backcrawl swimmers are far removed from the exponents of the old double-arm English backstroke with the frog kick. The simultaneous arm pull was shown to be less efficient than the alternate arm action, which maintained steady and even forward movement. In the last seventy years there have been many changes in technique but once more we get down to the problem of stroke laws, mechanics and physical ability. At the time of writing male backcrawl is the only stroke for which either American or American-trained swimmers do not hold the world record. The reason is Roland Mathes, a slim six-footer from East Germany. He defies all attempts by the rest of the world to dethrone him of his 100-metre and 200-metre world records. This young man is, in my opinion, the greatest swimmer in the world, a subjective assessment but one I hope to illustrate more clearly as I deal with the stroke.

An attraction of this stroke to beginners is that in the supine position breathing creates very few problems.

Body Position

A streamlined body parallel to the surface of the water is, once again, the ideal position for a backcrawl swimmer (figure

a   b

Figure 19

19a). The head is normally cushioned in the water with the eyes looking up towards the ceiling, or the sky in California. Because of the natural bend of the body swimmers have to be made aware of the importance of keeping their hips near the surface of the water and of not allowing them to sink into a sitting position (figure 19b). If the body is very buoyant it may be necessary to raise the head up by putting the chin down on to the chest to maintain a flat body position. Excessive movement of the head can create a large bow wave in front of the body, which inhibits forward momentum. The majority of backcrawl swimmers are very buoyant and the male tends to be tall and very lean. An assessment of the effectiveness of body position can be gained by studying the bow wave created by the body as it moves through the water. If the body lies high in the water the shoulders can be rotated to recover the arms without creating an excessive bow wave. An exceptional example of this point is shown by Roland Mathes, who creates very little resistance when he is in full stroke. The poor backcrawl swimmer who is trying to improve his stroke for medley swimming may find that he can maintain a high and parallel body position by arching his back slightly to keep his chest and hips high and kicking harder to keep the rear end of his body up.

Leg Kick

The alternate nature of the kick makes it easier to perform than the dolphin leg kick, because on land we walk and move about by using our limbs alternately. The purpose of the leg kick is to help to keep the body flat and stable while the arms propel it through the water. Although the feet are potentially larger paddles than the hands the legs do not have the mobility to use them in an efficient manner. If the body were completely

C

relaxed in the supine position and one of the legs were kicked upwards the reaction would be to drive the hips downwards. With both legs working alternately most of this action is cancelled out, but it is still important to tense the stomach muscles to stop the hips sinking, especially for the inexperienced swimmer. I am always surprised at the number of good backcrawlers who find difficulty in legs-only practice in driving their feet up to the surface and maintaining a flat body. The kick upwards is important if a swimmer wishes to develop a sound and steady body position. With the legs and feet extended one leg is kicked upwards while the other is pushed down. The kick starts from the hip and as the leg is moved upwards the knee bends and the toes are pushed backwards and down towards the bottom of the pool. The toes should break the surface of the water and on the downward movement should not sink too far below the body, or else they will cause considerable drag. Figure 20 shows how the toes turn back-

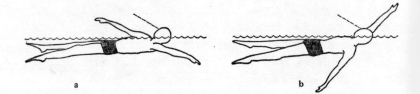

Figure 20

wards in the upward kick, especially if the swimmer's ankles are very flexible and the top of his instep is pointed directly backwards as in figure 20a and b, and give the body slight propulsion.

Arm Action

The arms should work alternately; as one arm is pulling the other is recovering over the water, thus producing continuous propulsive power. If the body is allowed to slow down the arms have to build up its speed again (overcome the body's inertia) before they can begin to move it faster; the body would thus be continually slowing down and accelerating. The arm enters the water behind the head fully extended, palm turned away from the body and the little finger entering the water first. Ideally the arm should enter the water very close to the head (figure 21a) and not as in figure 21b. Mobility of the shoulder joint will dictate where the arm enters, but in any case it should be lifted out of the water and recovered over the body, and should enter the water as close to the head as is humanly possible. Once the arm has sunk under the water the hand turns outwards (figure 21c) and the palm faces down towards the feet. The hand fixes in the water and the body is levered past by means of the muscles of the arms and upper body.

Figure 21e shows the path the hand takes as it searches for still water. During the pull the hand traces a path towards the feet and if the palm wishes to apply continuous backward pressure on the water the arm must bend. There are two distinct movements when the hand enters the water: it starts off by pulling the water and then once the elbow is behind it, it pushes backwards and down to the thigh. A backcrawler may recover by lifting his hand, thumb first, out of the water and throwing his arms straight up and over his body so that they hit the water, sink and pull and push without a pause. Figure 21d shows a back view of the bent-arm pull, which appears to be a very natural way of moving through the water. Research gives very strong indications that the bent-arm pull

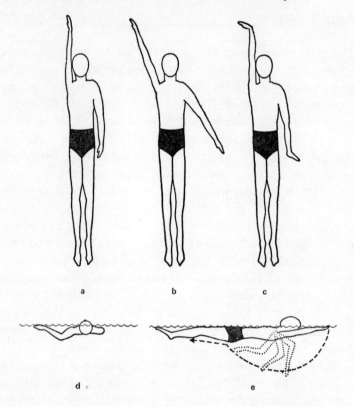

Figure 21

allows for the use of more muscles in the body, thus making the pull stronger and easier to perform. If youngsters had a complete understanding of what their hands should be doing in the water they could not help but perform a bent-arm back-crawl movement. The characteristic of Mathes's backcrawl is his long, slow-revving stroke; he has a very good 'feel' of the water and can probably move farther and faster on one arm pull than any other backcrawler in the world. It is no coincidence that the current British backstroke record-holder, Mike Richards of Wales, has also mastered the bent-arm pull and uses his long levers to great effect. He revs far more slowly than any other British backcrawler but each powerful arm pull drives his body along faster than his rivals. Richards is over six feet tall and is very lean, an ideal body shape for back-crawl. The recovery of the arms can create resistance problems if the swimmer lacks shoulder mobility, because ideally he should have the flexibility to recover his arms by lifting his shoulders out of the water and reduce frontal resistance in the form of a smaller bow wave. With the necessity for power in the pull there is going to be a certain amount of body roll where the swimmer leans into his pull, again to facilitate the use of more muscles in his body. This seems to be a natural reaction to the coach's demand for a stronger pulling action and, unless excessive, should not be eliminated. The 1968 Olympic 200-metre women's gold medallist 'Pokey' Watson was a good example of a swimmer who understood the power that could be derived from leaning into the stroke.

The straight arm backcrawl is still widely used in Britain, but it should be clear that it cannot possibly be as mechanically efficient as the bent-arm pull, where the hand is given a better chance of fixing itself in the water and acting as a fulcrum.

Breathing

In the supine position a backcrawl swimmer should have no problem in breathing, but it is desirable to create some sort of steady rhythm. Either explosive or trickle breathing is used, depending on the natural ability of the individual, but it is noticeable that most backcrawlers take in air through their mouths just as one arm is going into the water and blow out as the other arm goes in. Without being coached a swimmer will establish a breathing pattern, but it may not be the best method if it disturbs the rhythm of the stroke unduly. What is supposedly a natural movement can very often be the first attempt by an individual to bring some degree of success. Again, the art of coaching is highlighted: what must we change and what can we afford to leave alone? Initial success is not always the best method of measuring the effects of a new technique. It has been suggested that by holding the breath until the very last moment, as in explosive breathing, we improve the buoyancy of our body and make it rest higher in the water. This is very true, but whether the legs can keep the rear end of the body in the same high position or whether more resistance is created by the new position can only be a subject of conjecture. Application of these ideas and the effects on the individual are the only way in which we can justify any of them.

Timing

Although arms and legs may, at first, appear to work independently of one another, there is a definite rhythm between the two. When the right arm sinks into the water the body would keel over to the right if it were not for the ability of the left leg to kick downwards at the same moment. The same thing happens with both arms. One of the functions of the leg kick, then, is to put us in a position to kick downwards every time the opposite arm sinks into the water. It also has to keep the rear end of the body parallel to the surface of the water and to stop the legs moving apart and from side to side, thus causing excessive drag. Make a swimmer hold a float between his legs and swim backcrawl down the pool and the reaction of the arm movement will be seen in the sideways swaying of his legs. The body is no longer stable and streamlined, so the leg kick must be brought in and made powerful enough to cut down the body's resistance. If there is going to be any body movement it should be forward. The number of times the legs kick in a complete arm cycle varies from one individual to another; many use the orthodox six-beat kick, but a broken tempo version of this enables the arms to enter the water and work without pausing for the kick. The legs should 'dance a tune' to the arms. Four-beat leg kicks are the interpretation of some swimmers of the demand for better streamlining and balance, but whatever the rhythm it should never interfere with the power of the arm pull by using too much of the swimmer's limited body energy. The timing will vary, but we must always be on our guard to see that our leg kick is not interfering with our arms but is playing its role effectively.

Backcrawl Start

American collegiate swimming coaches are seriously consider-ing the merits of starting backcrawl races from the erect position on the blocks, as in all of the other strokes. Already their swimmers are allowed to start a race with their feet out of the water, which gives them an advantage in throwing their bodies backwards and over the water. The reader will see that under International Rules the competitor's feet must be under the water and that he must not stand in a gutter or curl his toes over the lip of the gutter. What an awkward way to start a race! I pray for the day when all races begin from a standing position on the pool-side and we can get rid of these ridiculous motorcycle handles from the starting blocks.

Figure 22a illustrates the position for starting a backcrawl race, the feet are placed firmly on the wall and comfortably apart to give minimum thrust. If a slippery wall is encountered it is sensible to make sure that one foot is lower down the wall than the other, so that if one foot slips the other is there to

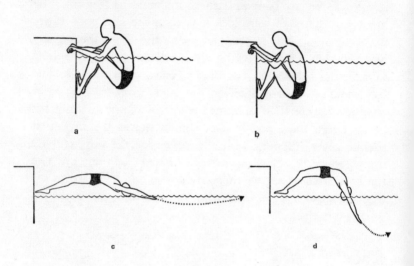

Figure 22

effect a push-off. The hands grip the handles at the side or under the starting blocks and the knees are usually bent and tucked up between the arms; I have seen instances of the knees being wide apart and the arms passing inside them, but I should have thought that it would be awkward to push off strongly if one's knees were wide apart. On the order 'Take your marks!' the arms bend, the body curls itself up and the face is brought close in to the block (figure 22b). It should be pointed out that there are many backcrawlers who do not pull their bodies close to the wall because they become too tightly cramped and cannot give maximum thrust on the wall with their legs. The length of legs and arms will dictate the ideal starting position. On the command 'Go!' the arms are thrown back over the head and the legs drive the body away from the wall (figure 22c). The objective is to lift the body over the water in a shallow backward dive and not just to push it through the water, which would create too much resistance to the forward motion of the body. Once the body has left the wall it should streamline itself and ideally the fingers should break the water first with the rest of the body following on behind. Swimmers should aim to allow the least possible area to come into contact with the surface of the water.

The body enters the water and continues to glide forward under the surface until it slows down to normal racing speed, when the head should break the surface and the full stroke begin. There are swimmers who prefer to start their leg kick before their arm action; as they are moving towards the surface they commence the kick and use one arm pull to complete the movement to the surface. It is very easy to enter the water too deeply, so that instead of shooting forward the body goes into a very deep supine dive. People with good shoulder and back mobility have a tendency to go into a supine pike position, as shown in figure 22d, and the consequences are clearly seen. In this case the swimmer throws his arms round the side of his body and head rather than over the top of the shoulders and the body responds by moving backwards rather than upwards. Highly flexible individuals should never throw their heads too far back and 'look for the water', because this can also cause a deep entry. As in any other starts practice should be designed to improve the power of the push-off and the streamlining the body. The average female swimmer can streamline her body far more effectively than the male but she normally has a much weaker push-off. A coach once told me that it was impossible to improve a particular swimmer's backcrawl start and turn so he was going to make him far fitter and faster than his rivals. The mind boggles at the picture of this individual outswimming his competitors down the length of the pool then allowing them all to catch him up on every turn; what utter frustration! A swimmer cannot afford to have real weaknesses like this because they will be exploited by his rivals.

Backcrawl Turn

'The competitor must not turn over beyond the vertical towards the breast before the foremost hand has touched the wall.' Once the touch is made the swimmer can do what he likes, as long as he is lying on his back when he pushes off from the wall. Again, the idea is to convert the forward speed of the body into a powerful thrust from the wall. An ability to turn on either hand is a great advantage because then the body can start to spin round some distance away from the wall. As soon as the leading hand touches the wall (figure 23a)

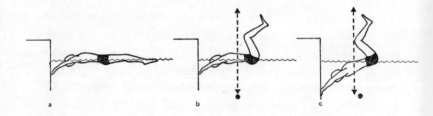

Figure 23

the head is thrown back, while the knees are drawn up towards the chest and together with the lower legs are lifted clear of the water (figure 23b). I like to see a backcrawler touch the wall under the surface of the water with his head already held back because it is then easier and quicker to lift the legs out of the water (figure 23c). The body also spins more easily the more vertical it becomes; anybody watching an ice skater will note how he can pirouette at a tremendous speed by drawing in his arms and standing in an erect position and then slow down again by extending the arms. By adopting this upturned but erect body position in backcrawl turn the body revolves quickly round its own axis and the feet are planted against the wall with the minimum delay. The swimmer should revolve his legs in the direction of his leading arm. A person with very long arms may find that he gets his feet on to the wall more quickly by touching with the leading hand, turning on to his front and performing a front somersault. We must always be prepared to experiment and exploit the rules to suit the individual.

The push and glide away from the wall should be powerful and streamlined, but it will not be if the body is allowed to come close to the wall, because the legs will be too cramped. I make no apologies for mentioning the turn of Roland Mathes. He lifts his lower legs and feet well clear of the water and spins round the shoulder of his leading hand. This part of his movement is noticeably slower than that of many other backcrawl swimmers, but once his feet are on the wall he develops a phenomenal push-off and breaks the surface well ahead of his competitors. A common fault is for a swimmer to touch the wall with his left arm and spin round his right shoulder. He should learn to turn round either shoulder, because his leading hand stabilizes his body while his other hand can help to spin it round. It is certainly the hardest turn to perfect and like all the others will become easy to perform only if the coach insists on correct turns in all training sessions. This is when a swimmer learns to turn on both hands. Far too many backcrawlers use grab turns in training and wonder why the correct turn seems slow in a race. Avoiding the problem will solve nothing.

4   Breaststroke

Captain Matthew Webb, the first person to swim the English channel, in 1875, used the breaststroke in achieving this monumental feat. Until recent years the breaststroke was considered the 'correct' method of moving through the water and Charles Newman,[1] the coach to Oxford University and Eton College, wrote in 1915: 'Far too little attention is given to the initial stages of swimming, and the pupil is apt to be slack and inaccurate. I am, therefore, not touching upon the fashionable or "fluke" strokes of which the "crawl" is the latest and fastest.' Even the backstroke, at this time, was a prone form of breaststroke with a frog kick. Breaststroke almost disappeared in the 1940s with the advent of the over-the-water recovery of the arms and the development of the butterfly stroke. In 1953 the two strokes were separated by new sets of rules. Nowadays the stroke bears no resemblance to the relaxed and flowing movements of the turn of the century. F. Holman of Great Britain won the 1908 Olympic 200-metre breaststroke event in 3 minutes 9.2 seconds and Brian Job won the 1970 American National Championship 200-metre event in 2 minutes 23.46 seconds. Japan, America and Russia have all left their mark on the development of the breaststroke, but fashions seem to have disappeared and all coaches are concerned with the best ways of applying proven mechanical principles. At the 1968 Olympic Games in Mexico I noted that all the Russian breaststrokes had varying leg kicks and body positions and it was clear that the strokes had been 'tailor made' to the individual.

Body Position

One part of the head should always break the surface and
the body must remain upon the breast with both shoulders on
a horizontal plane when swimming breaststroke. Because the
head has to travel high in the water it creates a reaction in the
lower body, making it sink (figures 24a and 24b). Two types of

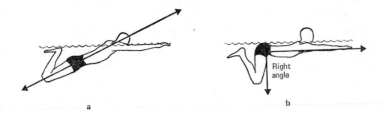

Figure 24

body position are shown in this diagram. In figure 24a the
hips are low in the water because in the leg kick the heels are
brought up and over the hips. The line shows the angle the
body makes with the surface of the water. Figure 24b illustrates a flatter body position where the hips are kept near the
surface of the water; in many cases this means hollowing the
back so as to keep shoulders and hips on the same plane. The
heels are either drawn up to the buttocks or drawn outside the
hips. In either case the body must be in such a position that
the heels do not come out of the water when kicking. Note that
the thighs form a right angle with the upper body and will
obviously set up resistance. Although figure 24a shows an
almost straight line between the upper body and thighs as
much resistance may be created as in figure 24b because the
body is so low in the water. The body position will depend
on the type of leg kick to be used and whether the head is

unduly lifted in the pull or breathing cycle. It has been my experience that some variation of figure 24b is the body position favoured by the majority of coaches and swimmers in the world.

Leg Kick

The nature of the leg kick allows for tremendous propulsion, unlike the other strokes where legs are used to streamline and stabilize the body. The amount of propulsion will depend upon the strength in the leg muscles and the mobility of ankle, knee and hip joints. A swimmer who naturally walks with his feet splayed outwards (at eleven and one o'clock) will have an advantage over those who walk with their toes pointing forwards or inwards. The feet, as well as the hands, are going to act as paddles, so big feet should be an advantage; Ian O'Brien, Olympic breaststroke champion for 1964, had size eleven feet and used them to great effect. Women have larger pelvic girdles than men and normally have a great deal more mobility in their joints.

From the legs-extended position the heels are drawn up towards the buttocks and the toes turn outwards (figure 25a and b). A very flexible individual may be able to draw his heels past his buttocks to the side of his hips while others may not

a   b   c

Figure 25

be able to reach the buttocks. The heels move apart to allow the feet to be drawn up as far as possible and the knees are

normally inside the feet (figure 25c). With the toes turned outwards the insteps of both feet are pointing backwards; this is
the area which is going to attempt to fix in the water and act as
a springboard from which the body can move forward. The
kick is begun by the swimmer pushing his feet backwards with
the heel leading so as to keep the instep pointing in a backward
direction. There will be an outward and rounded movement
of the legs depending on joint flexibility and their ability to
find undisturbed water to fix in. In the past I have often made
the mistake of forcing all swimmers to push the water directly
backwards, with the result that some have been unable to fix
their feet and derive any real propulsion. At the end of the
kick the legs come together and the toes should point and
streamline the legs to make maximum use of the propulsion
derived from the kick. To eliminate as much resistance caused
by the thigh as possible (figure 24b) the swimmer should be
encouraged to think of folding the lower leg over the top of the
thigh with the knee acting as a hinge. Care must be taken not
to break the surface with the feet but swimmers should keep
hips and feet as near to the surface as possible to cut down
unnecessary resistance. Ideally, the legs should not move out
of the line of the body and should remain near the surface
throughout. The legs will follow the line of the shoulders and
hips and if they are on the same plane, parallel to the surface
of the water, the feet will push the water backwards and will
not cause the body to lift out of the water. It boils down to
a swimmer's ability to apply Newton's third law of motion to
an area of still water, using a symmetrical and simultaneous leg
kick.

Arm Action

Starting with the hands together near the chin the arms are fully extended out in front of the body as the legs are kicked backwards. There may be a slight pause or glide before the arms are pulled (figure 26a) but this will be dealt with more fully in the section on timing. The hands are the paddles so they must 'fix' as quickly as possible. They are turned outwards and the arms move apart so that the palms are now

a   b

Figure 26

facing down towards the feet (figure 26b). The hands are pulled backwards and outwards but certainly not farther back than the shoulders, or else recovery of the arms will become slow and laborious. Perhaps a better idea can be given if the swimmer tries to lever his shoulders forward in the water and then just before they are level with his hands recovers his arms. The majority of male breaststrokers have a very powerful upper body and although the arm action is confined to a position in front of the shoulders it can be an extremely effective means of propulsion. Recovery of the arms takes place by the swimmer dropping his elbows and bringing his hands together. An easy way of dropping the elbows is to turn the palms of the hands upwards at the completion of the pull. When the hands come together under the chin they can be turned back over again before being extended to the next catch position. The reason for dropping the elbows and bringing them close together is to get the arms into a stream-lined position to derive full benefit from the strong arm action.

Breathing

Breaststrokers of old relied for the major part of propulsion on a very powerful leg kick and their arms and hands were used to help lift their head out of the water and make breathing a very easy action. Nowadays tremendous propulsion is gained from the arms and legs and a breath should be taken when there will be least interference to the efficiency of the stroke. The more the head lifts out of the water the more the stream-lining of the body will be affected, so a sensible point for swimmers to note is to keep the chin down in the water when breathing. The head should be lifted up by the neck and not by moving the shoulders, although I have seen many great breaststrokers who keep their head and shoulders very high in the water. If the body is almost parallel to the surface when we are swimming the stroke, our neck muscles should lift the head to breathe and the muscles in our upper body and legs should be concerned with driving the body forward. When the arms have completed the first half of the pull the head begins to lift and by the end of the pull inhalation has taken place. The head sinks back down into the water as the arms extend to complete the recovery. Those swimmers who use trickle breathing will start exhalation as soon as the face is back in the water while the explosive breathers will exhale halfway through the pull when their head begins to move upwards. Whatever type of breathing is used it should be executed in a smooth and steady manner.

D

Timing

The perfect breaststroker should derive just as much propulsion from the arm pull as from the leg kick. Imagine a swimmer with a weak leg kick: he surges forward on his arm pull but his leg kick cannot match the efficiency of his arms and his body slows down. Every time the arms function they will have to overcome the body's inertia and speed it up again. Ideally, the movements above and below the waist should each give the same thrust, so as to facilitate a smooth and steady forward movement. It is common to find a weakness in breaststroke amongst individual medley swimmers but closer inspection of the problem shows that it normally boils down to an inefficient leg action. In the best interests of the swimmer the weakness must be eliminated as quickly as possible. As an example, when Martyn Woodroffe swam against Gary Hall, the world record holder in individual medley, he was neck and neck with him through the first half of the race, but when they turned on to the breaststroke leg Hall took ten seconds off Woodroffe before turning onto the last 100 metres of front-crawl. That ineffective leg kick of Martyn's was his downfall at a vital point in the race.

Figure 27 illustrates the simplified form of timing in breaststroke. From the extended body position in figure 27a the arms begin to pull and as they reach the halfway mark the legs are drawn up to the buttocks; by the time the arms are recovered under the body and ready to extend (figure 27c) the legs begin their kick. As the legs thrust back the arms shoot forward and the front end of the body streamlines itself to take full benefit of the leg kick (figures 27d and 27e). The legs and feet come together at the end of the kick and the body may well glide for a fraction of a second before the next pull is begun. It is extremely rare to see a glide in a sprint swimmer

but it is very important that the arms are stretched forward
before taking the next pull. I believe that swimmers should
be more concerned with a stretch rather than glide of the body
at the completion of the leg kick. The ultimate in timing is
when a swimmer can fit the arm and leg movements together in
such a way that the body never slows down. A very practical
way of assessing efficiency in this is to look at the bow wave

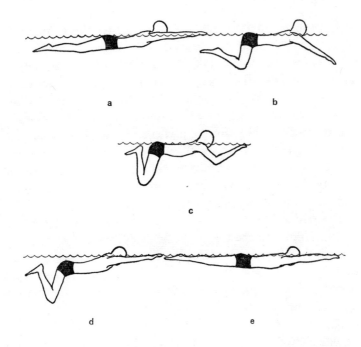

Figure 27

created by any breaststroker; if it remains at a constant height
the timing is good, but if it rises and falls, some part of the
body is weak and the legs and arms are retarding one another

by working at the wrong moment. When putting breaststrokers through a gruelling training session the coach should keep a close watch on any possible breakdown in the timing of the stroke and if this should occur the swimmers should either continue the session on another stroke or rest, because they will only become frustrated.

Breaststroke Start

After pushing off from the blocks a breaststroke swimmer is allowed to take one complete arm pull and leg kick under the water before his head breaks the surface to begin the stroke. The dive must, therefore, be deeper than for the other strokes because if not the body would come back to the surface before the actions of arms and legs were completed. It is impossible to lay down a particular angle of entry because some swimmers float better than others and will come to the surface sooner. The swimmer should aim to go as far down the pool as he possibly can and break the surface just as his body is slowing down to normal racing speed.

The position for starting on the blocks is exactly the same as for butterfly, with the feet comfortably apart and toes gripping the edge. Readers who are not familiar with this position should refer to the chapter on butterfly. On the command 'Go!' the swimmer topples forward and pushes off from the top edge of the block, entering the water in a streamlined position (see figure 18b) but in a slightly steeper dive. When he has slowed down to racing speed he takes one long arm pull right the way down to his thighs. The hands move in a large keyhole movement, starting by turning outwards and pulling round to the shoulders then moving in towards and finally under the body as the palms push the water backwards. As in full stroke, the hands act as a fulcrum to lever the body forward. At the completion of the arm action the hands are held on the thighs and the head is kept down with the eyes looking at the bottom of the pool. If the head is lifted the swimmer will move up towards the surface. During this powerful pull a dolphin-type reaction takes place in the extended legs and care must be taken to eliminate this by pushing the legs downwards, because vertical movements of the legs are contrary to breaststroke rules. A glide is held until the body begins to slow and then the hands and arms are recovered from the thighs by keeping them close to the stomach and chest to cut down resistance. At the same time the legs are drawn up to the buttocks and then kicked backwards as the arms are extended forwards from the face. All movements of the legs and arms must be simultaneous and symmetrical and the swimmer must remain upon the breast. No other arm or leg movement can be taken until the head has broken the surface of the water, so when the legs kick the head should lift slightly; the swimmer returns to the surface and full stroke begins.

It can be seen how important it is to time the leg and arm cycles to give maximum distance at maximum speed. Up until 1971 Britain lacked an intensive short-course swimming season where it was imperative for swimmers to have fast and efficient starts and turns to win races, and no other stroke lends itself to efficient starts and turns more than breaststroke.

Breaststroke Turn

The breaststroke is the slowest of the four competitive strokes and a swimmer cannot really afford to lose any momentum when he is turning. He must comply with the regulations and touch the wall with both hands simultaneously while remaining on the breast. Because the stroke is so slow it is essential for the swimmer not to glide into the wall; he should time the touch in such a way that his hands and arms are fully extended and the legs have just finished the kick. As soon as the touch has been made one hand is thrown away from the wall and the knees are brought up under the body to help speed up the movement of the feet onto the wall. The hand that stays on the wall acts as a fulcrum, allowing the legs to spin under it to the wall while the other arm and upper body move away and sink under the water. When the feet have been planted firmly on the wall the legs thrust the body away and the swimmer is once more streamlined to cut down resistance. It is important to note that once the feet have left the wall the body should be perfectly on the breast. As in the start, one underwater arm pull and leg kick is allowed. The ability of a swimmer to use his forward body momentum to place his feet quickly onto the wall is the important factor in determining turning efficiency.

There are a number of breaststrokers experimenting with the use of a forward somersault as in frontcrawl, but the problem here is to execute the two-handed touch on the breast and then have sufficient room and speed to perform a forward roll and plant the feet on the wall. Mark Carty, a current Welsh international breaststroker, has used this turn in major competition and I believe that his success is attributed to a short body which can rotate round its centre of gravity very quickly. It is very rare to see a competent gymnast over 5 feet 8 inches because the shorter person finds full body rotation easier to perform. Margaret Auton, ex-British Olympic swimmer, could tumble-turn to great effect in butterfly, but because the recovery of her arms was over the water she used to make such a splash with her hands that turning judges could never see whether she touched the wall with her hands or not. These two examples illustrate the case for experimentation by coaches and swimmers to find faster ways of turning without contravening the rules governing the stroke. International short-course events like the Bremen and Bonn competitions expose any turning weaknesses of swimmers, especially breaststrokers. A breaststroker who trains regularly in a short-course pool should have excellent turning ability because of the extra practice he gets at each repetition.

5 Frontcrawl

Frontcrawl is the most efficient method of moving through the water so far known to man. It is the only competitive stroke where the events vary in distance from 100 metres to 1,500 metres, making it necessary for the individual to adapt his style to suit the conditions of a particular race. The longer the distance swum the more concerned the swimmer is with economy of effort, although a close study of freestyle world records will show that the repetition times in all the distance events are very much the same. John Kinsella holds the world 1,500-metres world record of 15 minutes 57.1 seconds, an average of 61.5 seconds for the 100-metre laps. The lap time for the 400-metres record is only 60.5 seconds which, considering the variation in distance, is not all that different. A real speed differential is, however, seen over 100 metres, where the world record, held by Mark Spitz of America, is 51.9 seconds. In coaching frontcrawl consideration has to be given to developing a sprint stroke as well as a stroke which can be maintained for an extended period of time. The most common variation is in the leg kick, which will be dealt with more fully under the appropriate heading in this chapter.

Body Position

The mechanical requirements are the same as for the other strokes: body streamlined in the prone position and parallel to the surface of the water. Poise can be drastically altered by moving the head up and down in the water; the head should therefore be placed in such a position that the hips are near the surface. It is quite common to see women freestylers with their backsides breaking the surface of the water; if they dropped their heads the hips would be higher and the body would no longer be straight. Frontcrawl and backcrawl lend themselves easily to maintaining a streamlined body if care is taken to note the position of the head and hips. Johnny Weissmuller used to swim frontcrawl with his head held out of the water in the mistaken idea that his chest would aquaplane over the surface. The human body cannot move fast enough to derive any advantage from this theory and the swimmer must accept that he moves in the water and should attempt to cut his resistance down to a minimum. Figure 28 illustrates the ideal body position for a frontcrawl swimmer, but whether or not he can attain this will depend on many factors, such as distribution of body fat and the position of his head. A good sprint swimmer like Bobby McGregor or Mike Wendon clears the water with his shoulders and upper

Figure 28

back when moving at full speed, which necessitates a response from the lower body to match this new position.

Leg Kick

The leg kick has been the centre of controversy for many years, with its role in the full stroke being questioned by many people. It is universally accepted that the legs are used for stability and streamlining of the body and not for propulsion; they aid propulsion merely by cutting down body resistance. With the body lying on the front the alternate leg kick is executed in the same way as the backcrawl, except that the heels break the surface and not the toes. From the legs-extended position with the toes pointed one leg is pushed downwards while the other is moved upwards by the flexion of the hips. The pressure on the legs caused by the downward kick forces the knee to bend slightly and the toes to be pushed upwards (figure 29). The toes turn inwards and the legs stay

Toes pushed
backwards on down beat

Figure 29

close together to avoid causing any drag. The depth of the kick will depend very much on the degree of ankle flexibility but in any case it should not go too far under the body. The kick should be a rudder and stabilizer, not a sea anchor. Young swimmers can quickly master the downward kick but the upward movement calls for more strength and care has to be taken to see that they bring the legs back to the surface. How the kick fits into the arm cycle will be discussed in the section on timing the stroke. There is a tendency to neglect legs-only work in training because many coaches believe that, as it plays no major part in propulsion, the work would be wasted. Yet the muscles in the legs must be very efficient, because when they kick in the full-stroke action they must not divert valuable energy away from the arms. Sprinters need an efficient leg kick to keep the lower body in line with the high shoulders, so they cannot afford to neglect leg practice in training.

Arm Action

The alternate arm action of frontcrawl, like that in backcrawl, can give continuous propulsion so any body inertia as in butterfly can be eliminated. It used to be thought that the best way to use the arms was for one to be pulling while the other was recovering over the water, but film has shown that the recovery is faster than the pulling phase so the hands tend to catch one another up. Figure 30a shows the position where the right arm is beginning the pull but the left hand is still finishing its pull. How near the hands get to one another will depend on the individual's speed of recovery and his ability to hold the water. The entry of the hand into the water normally takes place, with the elbow held high, in between the shoulders and the head (figure 30b). It is important to keep the elbow

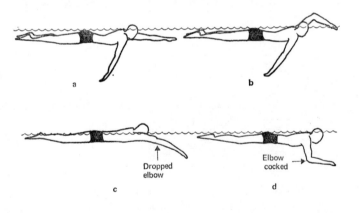

Figure 30

high and recover the arm by bringing over the shoulder close to the head. A low and rounded recovery can cause a reaction in the lower body and the legs will swing from side to side un-

less a more powerful and energy-absorbing kick is employed.
The fingers sink into the water and the arm stretches forward
under the surface until the hand reaches the catch position in
front of the body (figure 30c). The elbow should still be cocked
in this position because if it is allowed to drop and lead in the
pull (figure 30d) no leverage can be put on the hand and it
begins to slip in the water.

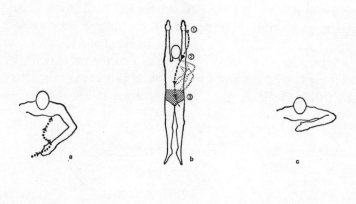

Figure 31

The palm of the hand faces back towards the feet and the
swimmer leans on this hand and attempts to lever his body
past it. The roll of the shoulders will allow more muscles to be
used in pulling. Figure 31 shows the path taken by the hand
as it seeks still water and pushes directly backwards. The first
half of the hand movement is a pull as the hand moves in a
rounded movement from in front of the shoulders to a point
under the body. The shoulder is now behind the elbow and
the hand is pushed backwards under the body to the thigh and
then is lifted out of the water with the elbow and recovered.

Figure 31c shows how much the elbow is bent and how close the hand can come to the body during the pushing phase. Male swimmers tend to roll their shoulders more than females because of their greater upper body strength, which can be used effectively only by leaning on to the hand.

The rate of turn-over will again depend on length of levers, strength and ability to fix the hand. Don Schollander was a freestyler who impressed coaches with his 'feel' of the water; his stroke turn-over was pretty slow but each pull was very powerful and the speed he obtained could more than match faster-revving rivals. On the recovery the arm should be relaxed with the back of the hand facing forwards, but just before entry the fingers should extend so that a solid paddle is placed into the water. How the hand goes in the water can affect the pull: a hand that is relaxed on entry may not become rigid in time to catch the first half of the pull and much leverage can be lost. Bobby McGregor was always relaxed in recovery but his arm entry was very precise because he realized that this affected the initial catch position. Australian swimmers have always been known for their low elbow and rounded recovery and certainly it has brought them a great deal of success in the past. Swimmers with poor shoulder flexibility have to use this type of recovery so once again a compromise of what the coach wants and what the swimmer can do has to be reached. As long as we are concerned with increasing the power of the arm leverage the stroke efficiency will be improved.

Breathing

With a stroke that is giving continuous propulsion choosing the ideal method and time to breathe can create problems. Whatever the method used it must not disturb the streamlining and propulsion. Again we come across the question of trickle or explosive breathing, but I have always left this problem to the swimmers themselves. I have no way of observing these swimmers under water so they may well be using a trickle method when I think they are breathing explosively.

As the opposite hand enters the water the swimmer should begin to turn his head and as soon as the mouth clears the water air is taken in and the head is returned to its normal position in the water. Care should be taken to turn the head sideways rather than to lift it because otherwise the legs could be forced downwards. The breath of air is taken in the trough behind the bow wave caused by the head, so very little movement of the head is required, especially if the swimmer is moving fast. If the head is turned when the opposite arm is entering the water, the breathing pattern fits in with the normal body role and at a point when one arm has not started pulling and the other has almost finished. Many coaches favour the use of bilateral breathing by their swimmers, especially if they are swimming distance events. This means that the swimmers are able to breathe to both sides; the head is turned to the right while the left arm starts to pull, then is returned to the water for one complete right and left arm cycle, and at the next right arm entry the head is turned to the left. I like to see swimmers doing this in training and distance races if the body is not unduly disturbed, but it is not always successful. Martyn Woodroffe had a terrible frontcrawl where his body twisted when he turned his head to the right to breathe. Even on bilateral breathing his body twisted when he turned to his natural side, so the problem was solved by allowing him to breathe to the left only. The body remained streamlined and the times came tumbling down. Frequency of breathing will depend on the distance being swum; sprinters breathe infrequently while distance swimmers use a regular pattern of either bilateral breathing or breathing on every stroke, to keep the muscles constantly supplied with oxygen.

Timing

After Karen Moras broke the women's 800-metres world record at the Commonwealth Games at Edinburgh in 1970, two swimming coaches came up to me and said: 'What's the matter with that girl? She didn't kick her legs.' Karen is a very buoyant swimmer with a high elbow recovery and her legs do not move from side to side or sink if she lets them trail. Here is an example of sound coaching where energy is not wasted on kicking when it is not necessary. The orthodox six-beat leg kick is not always the answer to timing in frontcrawl. Most of the finalists in the 1,500 metres in the Mexico Olympics kicked their legs twice to every one complete arm cycle whereas the sprinters were, in the majority of cases, six-beat kickers. Mike Wendon is a four-beat kicker over 100 metres but can slow the kick down over a longer distance. The problem is to establish a kick that will not interfere with the arm action but will maintain a flat and stable body. This can take the form of regular kicks of eight, six, four or two beats and irregular one-beat and five-beat kicks. When the head is turned in the breathing action many swimmers' legs cross over each other, either once or twice in the arm cycle. The leg cross-over can be a reaction to the arm recovery and it would be wrong to eliminate this for the conventional up-and-down leg kick. The legs are reacting to the arms and stabilizing the body.

Front Crawl Start

On the command 'Take your marks!' the swimmer moves to the front of the block and places his feet comfortably apart with the toes curled over the edge. The knees are bent and the body leans forward with arms stretched out in front and the head looking down the pool (figure 32a). The body is balanced on the balls of the feet and on the command 'Go!' it topples

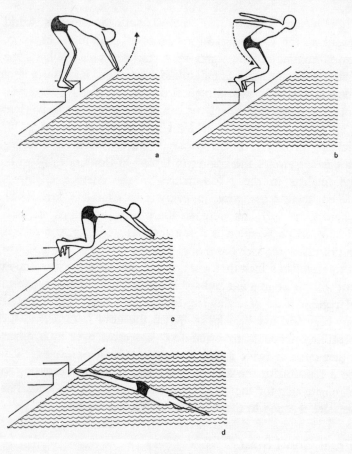

Figure 32

forwards and the arms drive backwards (figure 32b). The

arms swing forward as the toes exert pressure on the top side of the block (figure 32c). It was mentioned in the section describing the butterfly start that some swimmers swing their arms in a reverse circular movement, as shown by the dotted line in figure 32a. Any method of increasing the forward drive of the body is worth trying, although the same way may not suit everybody. On leaving the block the body streamlines and makes a clean shallow entry into the water (figure 32d).

As the body slows down to normal racing speed the legs can kick to help return the body quickly to the surface of the water before full stroke is begun. Perhaps the best example of the power that can be derived from an efficient start was Bobby McGregor's 100-metres final at the 1966 European Games. The gun went off before Bobby had assumed a good stance on the blocks and he was left behind. Exerting tremendous power on the top edge of the blocks with his legs he executed a clean and shallow dive and by the time his head broke the surface of the water again he was level with most of the other competitors. McGregor went on to win the gold medal and I've always admired his ability in that race to 'keep cool', although he may well have felt far from cool inside.

Frontcrawl Turn

The accepted way of turning in frontcrawl is the tumble turn or forward somersault with pike. As in the other strokes, British swimmers are very often as technically efficient as their American counterparts but they are very rarely as fast in execution. Having witnessed a number of American short-course meets I realize that swimmers with slow turns never reach the dizzy heights of champions. The best event illustrating the importance of speed is the 50-yards event in the National Collegiate Championships, which is swum in a 25-

E

yard pool. There is only one turn to perform, but a slight hesitation can lose a tenth of a second, which can mean the difference between first and last place. Britain does not yet have this intense type of competition which makes coaches and swimmers perfect turns. I paid particular attention to the ASA Championships at Blackpool in 1969 and 1970 and noted that the vast majority of freestylers would pick up their heads or slow down before reaching the wall. Admittedly the condition of the water was not conducive to good swimming, but the same swimmers were guilty of the same faults at the Commonwealth Games in Edinburgh. A foreign coach remarked to me that British swimmers were not confident of their turning ability because of lack of emphasis on turns in training. A junior British international, Sean Maher of Wales, trains in an 18-yard pool and because his coach, Mrs Hooper, puts great emphasis on fast repetitions in training, his turns have become very efficient.

The hands do not have to touch the wall in freestyle turns so the swimmer should take advantage of this by turning away from the wall and letting his feet touch and push the body off. Frontcrawl is also the fastest stroke, so if the fast forward speed can be converted into rotational speed the feet can be placed on the wall very quickly. I like to see the feet hit the wall with the legs tensed and slightly bent, as in figure 33d. The body should then rebound rather than push off in a slow and deliberate manner. Moving at full steam towards the wall the swimmer pikes the front half of the body (figure 33a and b) and, depending on the length of his legs, he may perform this action between two and four feet away from the wall. The heels and lower leg are brought out of the water (figure 33c) and swung over towards the wall. Meanwhile, under the surface the head should be looking back down the pool (figure 33b) and the trunk beginning to twist on to its side. If the right hand has led the body into the turn the twist should be under the left arm and on to the right shoulder. As soon as the feet hit the wall the body pushes off on its side with the hands moving

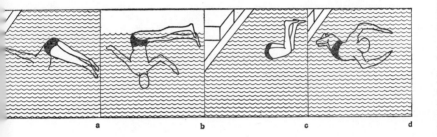

a   b   c   d

Figure 33

forward and streamlining in front of the head (figure 33d). When the feet have left the wall the body rolls over onto its front and glides forward and towards the surface until the kick and full stroke are started.

Problems arise when swimmers cannot turn on either hand: they have to slow their body down and make adjustments before reaching the wall. The turn must become fluent and swimmers should be encouraged to turn on either hand even if they make initial mistakes in training. I have known many swimmers who have learnt to turn, say with their left hand leading, but instead of performing the half twist under the right shoulder, they still move to the left. A method common amongst South African swimmers involved letting one hand catch up with the other just before the turn and a powerful butterfly pull was used to speed up the body rotation. There is certainly a delay in the stroke as the hands are adjusting and it is doubtful whether the increase in turning speed compensates for the slowing down of the stroke. A common mistake in the turn is for swimmers to bring their knees up to their chest rather than bringing their lower leg out of the water. The turn is performed in a pike and not a tuck position. Once technique and ideal turning distance from the wall have been mastered speed is the most important factor to work on. Mike Wendon performs a peculiar type of turn, a cross between a backcrawl spin turn and a reverse somersault and he has been a world sprint record holder. I pose the question: 'Would he be even faster with a tumble turn?'

6 Physiology of Training

Every swimmer and coach knows that the body is put under tremendous stress in competitive swimming and that success will be realized only if the body can function efficiently under these conditions. To be fit is to be adapted for some specific activity and thus it is true to say that a swimmer is not necessarily fit for squash or cross-country running. How many times have I heard people talking about their daily two-mile walk which is making them fit. Fit for what? It just means that their body has adapted to the stress of the walk and they no longer find it a strain. There will certainly be some carry-over to other activities, in that the person may find that he begins to lose weight and increases his muscle tone. Swimming training has become such a long and laborious daily task that we cannot afford to waste time on activities which will not cause specific adaptations.

The human body is so complex that it is impossible to know the best way of improving the efficiency of all functions used in swimming. Where science can tell us no more we must rely upon intuition based on previous experience. World-renowned coaches such as Forbes Carlile of Australia and Doctor Councilman of the United States have the facilities and the academic training to do research into the physiology of training. Lesser mortals rely upon the distribution of all this research information, but its interpretation into practical use is the real, crucial issue. In Britain many 'boffins' are doing research into exercise but none of these people are involved in the daily coaching of competition swimmers, so the results of their work can be assessed only in the light of practical experience. A year before the 1968 Olympic Games in Mexico, Britain sent a team of physiologists and athletes to study the effects of altitude on training and competition. The results and recommendations were distributed to all the sports bodies and the swimmers were strongly advised to take things easy during the first week in Mexico City. Everybody had an 'altitude phobia' and when they quickly became tired during light training they tended to take things far too easy. It was my experience that repetition times were slower and swimmers found the work harder, but that was no excuse for resting. If coaches and swimmers had worked with the scientists in 1967 many of the fears would have been eliminated and the swimmers would have been more inclined to work harder. In contrast, the Australian team accepted tough work-outs because they had had previous experience of working hard under similar conditions. In Britain's case, theory and practice had not been united for the common good.

Before we study the physiology of training we should look at some of the components that go to make up a competitive swimmer:

1 Technical skill (ability to perform the strokes efficiently)
2 Strength (see chapter 8)
3 Cardiovascular and muscular endurance
4 Flexibility (see chapters 1 and 8)
5 Personal ambition and adroitness (see chapter 7)

Bert Kinnear, the ex-Senior National Technical Officer in England, was instrumental in drawing up the above components and I have used them as a firm basis for laying down training schedules. This chapter will be concerned with the endurance of heart and muscles.

Forbes Carlile[2] has described the stress concept and outlined the work done by the Canadian Dr Hans Seyle on the General Adaptation Syndrome. Seyle reported that if parts of the body were put under stress, e.g. the muscles, there would be specific effects in the muscles and more general effects over the whole of the body. The body reacts to a particular stress by setting up a resistance mechanism, but as it nears the stage of exhaustion its resistance gradually decreases. Every body is assaulted by all kinds of stresses, microbes, diseases, nervous tensions, physical exercise and so on, and must accumulate a store of energy to adapt to the pressures. Each individual has a different amount of adaptation energy and therefore differing amounts of training or stress can be taken. This does not mean to say that certain swimmers should take training easy because it hurts them; rather they should consider reducing the other stresses upon their body by ensuring adequate rest, good diet and so on. It is interesting to note Councilman[3] reporting on the amount of sleep that some of his university swimmers take: the hours vary from six to twelve, showing that individual requirements vary considerably.

Besides working the swimmers through progressively tougher training programmes, the coach must keep a continuous watch for signs that the individual is not adapting properly to the stresses put upon him. Symptoms of failing adaptation are loss of weight, irritability and insomnia, all of which are soon spotted by a coach who has a very good relationship with his team. A swimmer who reaches the exhaustion stage poses a serious problem to the coach: should he rest the swimmer completely or hope that the effects will wear off? The correct answer is to find the cause of the failing adaptation; it may, for instance, be nervous tension caused by examinations or personal problems, or the body may be using its supply of energy to repel an attack of influenza. Whatever the problem, the coach must be ever-vigilant to keep his athletes in a position where they can respond to the work he is giving them. Failing adaptation has always been a serious problem when preparing British teams for major competitions like the Olympic Games. Swimmers come together who have tremendous differences in their training backgrounds, some having swum seven miles a day while others have covered only seven miles a week. The weaker members cannot possibly benefit from an intensive programme in two or three weeks and work must be set that will encourage all concerned to work and obtain the best possible adaptation in the shortest possible time. Again, we illustrate the ability of the coach to apply work which has a scientific basis. A coach may have all the technical know-how but if he cannot create the environment in which the swimmer will respond the knowledge is useless. Chapter 7 will highlight this problem of creating a sound working environment.

Mark Spitz is the present holder of the world 100-metres freestyle record of 51.9 seconds. Ideally we should like to have a swimmer maintaining such a pace over longer distances. If we can swim 100 metres in 51.9 seconds why can't we swim 400 metres in (4 × 51.9) 3 minutes 27.6 seconds? A careful study of present world records will show that this sort of thing is happening. Swimmers are becoming so well conditioned that they can swim long distances at a very fast pace. We are reaching the stage where distance events mean a long sprint. Below is a list of world freestyle records up to December 1970, with the average pace for each distance. Dawn Fraser's 100-metre world record has stood since 1964 but all others have been smashed during the last two years. Those marked with an asterisk were broken in 1970, which shows that swimmers' conditioning must be improving. A further comparison of this list and other world records with those of current British records will show just how far behind the rest of the world Britain is; if the position is to improve British swimmers must be made to undergo a steadily increasing stress programme.

Men

NAME	DISTANCE	TIME	PACE
* Mark Spitz (USA)	100 m	51.9	51.9
Don Schollander and			
Mark Spitz (USA)	200 m	1.54.3	57.1
* Gunnar Larsson (Sweden)	400 m	4.02.6	60.6
Mike Burton (USA)	800 m	8.28.8	63.6
* John Kinsella (USA)	1,500 m	15.57.1	63.7

Women

NAME	DISTANCE	TIME	PACE
Dawn Fraser (AUS)	100 m	58.9	58.9
Debbie Mayer (USA)	200 m	2.06.7	63.3
* Debbie Mayer (USA)	400 m	4.24.3	66.0
* Karen Moras (AUS)	800 m	9.02.4	67.8
Debbie Mayer (USA)	1,500 m	17.19.9	69.3

British coaches should be planning the work over years and not on a monthly basis. I am reminded of the story of a British coach who told me of the programme that his swimmers were going through. He said that the squad was handling the work-load very well and training times were falling but there was no appreciable improvement in competition. The point was that the swimmers had completely adapted to the work of the coach and there was no increase in the stress put upon them. Once a person has completely adapted to a particular stress he needs to be exposed to greater pressures if further adaptation and improvement in competitive performance is to take place. This was not happening in this case and the swimmers were becoming disillusioned with the training and the coach. Over the last ten years a number of swimmers from all over the world have gone to the United States in the hope of finding the secret of swimming success. They have all found that it is based on a hard, progressive work-load that many of them have found too difficult to handle. Some, like Hans Fassnach of West Germany, have responded well and have in no time at all broken a world record.

How do we decide the quantity and quality of work for each individual? It is my belief that young swimmers should have the initial aim of becoming technically proficient in all the strokes and the appropriate starts and turns. A progressively tougher training programme can then be given to them to see how their bodies respond, based on the idea that they are all training to become multi-distance medley swimmers. This does not involve specialization as sprinters or distance swimmers but just a basic grounding in physiological conditioning. As they become more mature swimmers they can specialize in particular events and their training can become more specific.

At the beginning of this chapter I mentioned the components of a competitive swimmer. I now intend to apply the General Adaptation Syndrome to the improvement of cardiovascular and muscular endurance.

Cardiovascular and Muscular Endurance

The muscles of the upper body require a constant supply of oxygen and glycogen if they are going to work efficiently when pulling the body through the water. During exercise glycogen is released into the blood stream and transported to the muscles by the blood. In the trained athlete a reserve supply of glycogen is stored in the liver for any emergency. Blood also transports the oxygen from the lungs to the muscles and takes away the waste products of exercise such as carbon dioxide. The chemistry of the blood and muscles is a most fascinating subject and I would encourage the interested reader to study the subject in greater depth. Without an efficient supply of materials the muscles cease to work and, for this reason, an efficient flow of blood is of paramount importance. The heart, which is just a large pump, controls the rate of flow of the blood and a major problem is to make it send greater quantities to the working muscles. Exercise increases the heart-rate so that more blood is pumped through to the muscles, but under intense pressure the heart can pump so fast that it becomes completely inefficient: each heartbeat squeezes only a fraction of the normal amount to the muscles and thus the blood supply is drastically reduced. Ideally, the chambers of the heart should fill completely with blood before it is squeezed out through the aorta into the arteries and then any increase in the rate at which this function can be performed will greatly enhance the work-output of the muscles. When the blood reaches the muscles it passes down, via capillaries (fine blood vessels), through the sheets of muscle taking oxygen and glycogen to every muscle fibre. Certain types of exercise can improve the efficiency of capillaries within the muscles because it is no use having plentiful supplies of oxygen and glycogen being transported to the muscles if they cannot pass through the muscle to the fibres. Interval training improves the muscles of the heart by a series of efforts which gradually make the heart adapt by beating more slowly but more powerfully, thus sending a greater volume of blood to the muscles on each beat. The heart is a very difficult piece of machinery to keep under pressure because it is so well protected by the muscles of the body. When it is put under too much pressure the muscles become tired and cease to work; the heart can then put the body back to normal and take a rest.

Most physiologists agree that if the heart is working at 150 beats per minute (bpm) or more it will gradually adapt to this pressure and begin to function more efficiently. In interval training I like to see swimmers finishing a repetition with a pulse rate of 160 bpm or more, but this will depend very much on the individual and a uniform number cannot be given. Interval training is best applied over varying distances with short rests and a steady pace. An example would be a swimmer whose best 100-metre freestyle time is 60 seconds dropping down to 75 to 80 per cent of his best time when repeating 10 x 100-metre swims, with a 20-30-second rest between each repetition. This would give a pace of 72 to 75 seconds and the pulse could easily be taken by the swimmer. If the pulse remained at 120 bpm (which is highly unlikely), then pace or resting interval could be changed to increase the pressure. A word of caution to any swimmer who thinks that he can get straight into the water and perform eight miles of interval work in his first session: the results will be disastrous. He may have a struggle to cover ten fifties with a short rest in some sort of reasonable time. The particular stroke used will also affect the result: it is much harder to train on butterfly than freestyle, so commonsense must prevail. We must learn to walk before we can run.

Here are some examples of interval-type training used by Martyn Woodroffe. By interval training I mean efforts of equal intensity which have an effect upon the cardiovascular system.

20 x 50 metres	freestyle	every 45 seconds	average 35 seconds
10 x 400 metres	freestyle	every 5 minutes	average 4mins 45secs
10 x 200 metres	butterfly	every 3 minutes	average 2mins 30secs

Note the longer resting interval (30 seconds) on the butterfly stroke. Many 'purists' will argue that this is not real interval training, but I wanted Martyn to perform work which affected the cardiovascular system and short resting intervals seemed to be the answer. During the resting intervals his pulse would drop from 180 to 140 bpm, which seemed to be ideal at the time. Other swimmers in the squad would have either longer rests or shorter repetitions, depending on the conditions prevailing. Rather than write a schedule down and adhere to it rigidly I prefer to say to myself that I want the swimmers to experience the effects on the heart and I will then present the work according to ability with the object of obtaining common results. Short-rest training can become very boring, but it will be seen in chapter 7 that the work can always be related to particular races or parts of races.

How much of this type of training should be done will depend largely on the particular event a swimmer is aiming for. Bobby McGregor would never do much of it because he was not interested in any race over 100 metres and therefore concentrated on work that would improve his speed. Martyn Woodroffe spent three-quarters of his time working on this type of programme to ensure a constant blood supply to the muscles over his 400-metre individual medley and 200-metre butterfly events. When setting out a work-out of this type I prefer to give a time limit to each repetition, such as 10 x 50 metres every 45 seconds, rather than 10 x 50 metres with a 10-second rest. I find that the time limit makes swimmers conscious of finishing their repetition in under 45 seconds to take a rest and the quality of their work appears to improve. With a guaranteed 10-second rest they could take it easy on each repetition and cover the 50 metres in 45 seconds. But the other way the pressure is on them to finish the work as quickly as possible.

Perhaps the greatest improvement in British training over the last ten years has been in the amount of work covered in the same period of time. Schedule A illustrates a work session of 'yesteryear' and B the look of the seventies. In the seventies an accomplished swimmer can cover the same quantity of work (4,000 metres) in one hour as opposed to two, and there will not be all that much difference in the repetition times, especially over 50 metres. As the swimmer becomes fitter either the quantity per hour can be increased or the speed of repetitions, or a combination of both. Chapters 9 and 10 will show how the individual's needs are catered for and how the coach assesses the quantity and quality of training. Moderately fast work with short rests should improve circulation, muscle capillarization and, in some cases, the size of the heart. The only way of objectively measuring the effects of certain types of training is in the results of races or time trials. Short rests produce an average pace of training and this type of work would be ideal for 400- and 1,500-metre swimmers.

A

20 x 100 metres	freestyle	every 4 minutes
40 x 50 metres	freestyle	every 1 minute
Total time: 2 hours		

B

20 x 100 metres	freestyle	every 1½ minutes
40 x 50 metres	freestyle	every 45 seconds
Total time: 1 hour		

The lactic acid produced by the muscles during exercise must be neutralized by the alkali reserves carried in the blood or else the muscles will seize up. Trained swimmers can stand a higher blood alkalinity than people leading sedentary lives and it is thought that they produce large quantities of alkaline reserves in the body. Some researchers believe that faster interval training, where longer rests are given, will have a good effect upon the muscles pulling the body by making them used to working without oxygen and keeping the lactic acid level down by using the alkaline reserves. Readers may recall the example of Woodroffe performing twenty 50-metre swims every 45 seconds averaging 35 seconds in the slower interval training. By repeating every 1¼ minutes his average time would drop to 32 seconds, showing that the effects of the work would be directed towards the muscles. Although I have no way of proving it, I do believe that the faster interval training does improve the muscles' ability to work with a high lactic

acid content. I do not like to see a competitive swimmer training at a pace below 75 per cent of his racing speed because,
although this may improve cardiovascular endurance, it
encourages a swimmer to adopt a pace which bears no resemblance to racing speed and a different stroke technique may
be 'grooved' into the individual.

Muscular Strength

The faster the training becomes, the greater the effect on the
ability of the swimmer to sprint. This ability is closely related
to the strength of the upper body muscles and besides the use
of land conditioning, the muscles can be strengthened by using
repetition and sprint training. If sprinting relied on muscular
strength alone, we should see weight-lifters performing miracles
of swimming speed. Repetition and sprint work strengthen the
muscles, while at the same time the individual is benefiting
from the kinaesthetic sense of moving at a very fast pace.

The Choice of Material

Before dealing with how a coach and swimmer select the type
of work to use, the table below of the four basic types of training should be studied. It is based on a swimmer whose best
100-metre time is 60 seconds and who performs 10 × 50-metre
swims with varying rests.

Type of training	Effort per cent	Resting interval	Pace (secs)	Effect
Sprints	95+	2–3 minutes	29–31	Improves sprint
Repetition	90–95	1–2 minutes	31–33	Improves sprint
Fast interval	85–90	½–1 minute	33–35	Improves sprint and endurance
Interval	75–80	5–10 seconds	35–37	Improves endurance

The best method of applying this table to a swimmer is to take two examples:

Swimmer A A girl of sixteen with a best time for 100 metres breaststroke of 83.5 seconds wishes to improve her sprint and break 80 seconds in the following year. After a careful study the coach finds out that she has broken 40 seconds for 50 metres on only two previous occasions. In other words, she cannot sprint but has the endurance to swim a steady pace during the race. Perhaps some coaches would settle for a steady build-up of the two interval-type training programmes followed by a couple of months' hard repetition and sprint work before the big competition where she wants to break the elusive 80-second barrier. I certainly would not neglect the build-up of endurance work but, because her problem is an inability to sprint, it should be tackled immediately. About 25-30 per cent of her winter build-up would consist of repetition and sprint work because a sign of improvement will encourage any swimmer to work harder in all spheres of training. We cannot adhere to a particular set of rules without considering the individual's problems and adjusting the rules to suit the swimmer. The truly great coaches have a flair for developing talent in all their swimmers.

Swimmer B The boy is fourteen years old and although he has swum 100 metres freestyle in 61.5 seconds he cannot break five minutes for the 400 metres. Straight away, the coach can see that the boy has the speed but not the endurance to go with it over 400 metres. The bulk of this individual's work will consist of interval training and repetition work. A target of 4 minutes 40 seconds is set as the time to be achieved in the following year, which when broken down to 4 seperate 100-metre swims gives a pace of 70 seconds, or 35 seconds for 50 metres. Training can be directed towards achieving sets of these target times which, if successful, will add greatly to the swimmer's interest in his work. Sprints will never be completely neglected because they are a great source of motivation, but in this swimmer's case they will take a back seat.

Later chapters will deal with the planning of the year and the type of work to be covered but already it can be seen that training can no longer be a hit-and-miss affair. We must critically assess the effects of our work each year and look for the weaknesses in the programme. The combination of sprinting and endurance training is important in any programme, but it is no use trying to repeat the programmes of previous years because the results may never improve. As in motor racing, we have to look for better combinations of technical knowledge; we must never become complacent and hope that our present techniques will always bring success. How the scientific facts are implemented will show the ability of a coach or swimmer.

F

7   Psychology of Training

In my schooldays I came into contact with many teachers who had a tremendous knowledge of their subject but who somehow found great difficulty in passing on information to their pupils. This lack of communication was the downfall of many a teacher and student. Similarly, swimming coaches may have all the technical know-how at their fingertips, but if they cannot turn it into swimming success their knowledge can bring only personal academic satisfaction. The coach could be likened to the technologist who turns pure science into its practical form of aeroplanes, bridges or computers. Perhaps a better title for this chapter would be the application of psychology to swimmers, because that is really what coaching is all about. Later chapters will deal with the role of the coach and swimmer in training but here we are concerned with the best way of motivating the swimmer.

What is motivation? An easy answer is the drive or degree of activity a person displays. Lovell[4] defines motivation as an internal process, initiated by some need, which leads to activity that will satisfy that need. He goes on to say that we also have incentives, which are administered by external causes, and which often determine the nature and direction of human activity. In other words, we may have only a luke-warm drive to be successful in a certain activity but this can be strengthened by adding incentives in many and varied forms. A certain swimming club in Wales experienced great difficulty in finding fixtures and in one particular year had only two matches. The swimmers began to drop away and take up other activities. What was the point of training every day, they argued, if they were never going to see the fruits of their labours in the form of competition? The external incentives were non-existent and only the very dedicated individuals continued to train in the hope that things would improve.

We will return to motivation later in the chapter but let us now highlight some of the problems facing swimmers when they are trying to improve their stroke technique and general level of swimming fitness. Swimmers are not 'zombies' who can be put through hours of tortuous training sessions day after day. They are individuals who are ever-conscious of the stresses put upon them and the coach must be fully aware of this fact. The competent coach will measure his own ability to improve the swimmer's condition by studying the results of his labours in terms of his pupil's improved performance. The world of education is continually searching for better ways of acquiring skills, be they mental or physical.

I am convinced that there are teachers who believe that youngsters learn new skills only if they are given directions or shown a film. Pugelski[5] summed this up well when he said: 'Learning is done by the learner and not by some kind of transmission process from the teacher.' The learner must experience the new stresses of a situation if he is going to learn anything at all, so how can we make all of our training sessions more effective? It is my belief that every work-out should have a theme and an aim that is within the scope of each individual in the squad. Even in the preparation period, which could be months away from the important competitive phase, the swimmers can be encouraged to take an intelligent interest in their training. This period is ideal for improving their stroke technique but how best to present the work poses a large question mark. A few important factors which affect the learning process are discussed in the next few paragraphs.

Is it better for a swimmer to improve his technique by practising without advice or instruction or is learning increased by giving advice? If the learner is left to himself he normally continues to practise the first method to bring him success, though this can often be technically unsound. The swimmer therefore needs somebody who can measure his work in an objective manner and keep him informed of the effects of his work. Those who are left to practise without knowing the results are unlikely to improve their performance. Knowledge of bad points breaks down old habits and knowledge of good points builds up new habits. Criticism is used sparingly to create dissatisfaction with the swimmer's current stroke while praise helps build up the new one. Films can help only if the coach is able to pick out the critical points of the stroke, because the less important ones could give the swimmer the wrong 'feel' of the movement. The same applies to verbal instructions, where emphasis on unimportant points can only lead to confusion. What we are really searching for is a method of improving stroke technique as soon as things begin to go wrong. A swimmer may be asked to swim one length of a twenty-five-metre pool paying attention to a particular technical point; if he performs the movement incorrectly there is no way of informing him until he has completed the length of the pool. The best example of 'instant correction' is shown on the front of Dr Councilman's book *The Science of Swimming*, where we see the 'Doc' standing in front of an underwater observation window in his pool with microphone in hand. He can see the swimmer clearly, performing frontcrawl, and is able to relay information via the underwater sound apparatus directly to him the instant his technique breaks down. This is the ideal situation, but even this method could prove useless if complicated and irrelevant directions were transmitted. One set of directions may suit one person but may not trigger off the chain of events for another person to acquire the desired skill. Age can also affect the rate at which a person learns a skill and, as many skills are very complex, intelligence can play an important part in his ability to acquire or improve new techniques. The individual is a complex being and his response, be it negative or positive, should be an important indicator of a coach's ability to communicate. I like to conceive a coach's role as that of a catalyst: a person who alters the rate at which the reaction of swimmers to training occurs. He has to create a situation where swimmers cannot help but learn and improve. When handling large groups this is an almost impossible task, but it should still remain the ultimate goal in the mind of the coach.

An example of the application of psychology to training by a coach was the role I played with a young Welsh backcrawl swimmer. He was having great difficulty in improving his sprinting ability, even though he was performing a good deal of tempo and high-quality work. Frustration was setting in and he was fast becoming disillusioned with swimming and training in a 55-yard pool, where his fastest one-length sprint had been 34 seconds. We spent a week training in a 55-foot pool and I saw this as the solution to the problem, because he now found that he could sprint one length in under 10 seconds. I then convinced him that he had a considerable sprinting ability and my argument was reinforced when I made him do three one-length (55 feet) sprints every 15 seconds, each in under 10 seconds. It gave him a tremendous boost to know that he had the ability to do so and that it could well be lack of strength or endurance which stopped him from performing this sort of time in the 55-yard pool. Given more time I would have strengthened his faith in himself by reducing his resting time by two or three seconds. There was a carry-over to the bigger pool, where his 55-yard sprints improved by two seconds.

An important part of motivation is self-improvement because this creates an interest in the particular activity, as was the case in the above example. If the coach can create a situation where success is an inevitable consequence of hard work on the part of the swimmer then his motivation will be strengthened.

Peter Daland, coach to the University of Southern California, once told me that one of his big coaching problems was to make swimmers admit to themselves that they had certain weaknesses. The natural reaction was for the swimmer to defend himself against the verbal onslaught of the coach instead of accepting the constructive criticism. If the relationship of swimmer and coach is strong then the swimmer will soon admit his weakness and the necessary remedial actions can be taken. An example is that of a coach who tells a swimmer that his turns are slow and the reply may be: 'I can't see the wall.' This is not satisfactory because, if this is the case, the swimmer will have to learn to turn fast in spite of his inability. If the turn is slow the coach and swimmer must work together to overcome the many hazards which are retarding the swimmer.

There are swimmers who spend as much as four hours per day in the water and one of the greatest problems is boredom. Lack of variety in the work is the prime cause of swimming boredom and the coach is forever searching for new methods to motivate his squad. It has already been mentioned that success is crucial to an individual's future involvement in a particular activity, although there are many exceptions to this rule because some individuals have more internal desire to succeed than others. The mind boggles at the number of actors and artists who are prepared to live in extremely poor conditions for years in the hope that their talent will bear fruit. They have faith in themselves and their ability to succeed. But even the strongest characters have their weak moments and the coach will vary the work accordingly. Things often go wrong during an important time of the year and it is a problem to know whether a swimmer's work pattern should be changed or whether a complete rest is desirable, with the consequent decline in physiological conditioning. The rest may well reinvigorate the individual and the way he attacks the training after a rest will soon restore his old level of conditioning, besides increasing his psychological fitness. An ever-changing and individually challenging swimming programme will go a long way to keeping serious problems to a minimum. In 1967 Leo Hendry[6] led a discussion of coaches, swimmers and parents at the ASA National Championships in Blackpool. He reported that swimmers were clearly affected by the distance of repetitions in training. Their favourite training distance was 25 yards, so perhaps more repetition work should be done over this distance. Now coaches may say that if swimmers like working over 25 yards they will put more effort into their work, so it seems sensible to make this an important distance in training. I would not agree, because the swimmers could become just as bored with this distance as with any other. The answer really is to note this recommendation and integrate this 25-yard swim into a training plan. It should be used but not abused.

How can young swimmers lead a normal life and plough up and down the pool for six or seven days of the week? The answer is a desire to succeed in spite of the hardships, which then develops a high degree of self-discipline. Karen Moras, the Australian distance freestyler mentioned in earlier chapters, rises at 4.30 a.m. to get down to the pool for a two-hour training session before school. Besides fitting in the training a swimmer must maintain the necessary scholastic standards at school and have some time each day to relax and pursue other interests. During my North American tour in 1969 many university coaches told me that their swimmers experienced academic difficulties during those periods of the year when they were doing little training. When they were training hard they programmed their day rigidly to fit in study, training and other activities. They responded well under pressure and imposed an efficient form of self-order to see them through this trying period. British swimming is now alive to the problem of providing training facilities for children just before and just after school. Gone are the days when successful swimmers trained from nine to ten each evening. The swimmer who finishes his daily work-outs by seven every evening will have time to settle down to home-work and recreational pursuits. The idea of pursuing an activity to the virtual exclusion of all others is contrary to the ideals of many educationists in Britain today, but I can see nothing but good coming out of the experience if the decisions are made by the swimmer and not by parents or other interested parties. Very rarely do we see clubs which genuinely cater for adolescent swimmers by providing a social environment that will hold their interest as they pass through this awkward stage in their development. A coach cannot afford to run a swimming factory; if he wants to get the best response from the older swimmers he must offer them work and social involvement which is relevant to their development.

The hours of training are long and can often become boring, especially if the coach is not alive to his job. We cannot get away from the truth that success is the result of sound planning and hard work. The swimmer who can be made to put his heart and soul into every training session will eventually be more successful than the swimmer who works hard only on odd occasions. How the work is done is more important than what is done. Chapter 9 discusses the planning of the swimming year but I feel it is important to discuss a part of this

topic here. A swimmer must never be allowed to lose sight
of the aim of all his hard work. I have even met swimmers
who enjoy training but not competition. This competitive
aim, be it success in the national championships or a new
record time should always be present in the application of
psychology to the individual. It is no use saying to a swimmer that a particular form of work is improving his power of
endurance if this cannot be shown in the form of a time trial
or simulated swim. The work must always bear resemblance
to the racing situation, yet with training becoming ever more
technical it is easy to lose sight of this objective. Up until 1971,
Britain had only a one-season year, starting with the British
Trials in March and finishing some time in September with
the Olympic or European Games. In the period from October
to March it was easy to lose interest in training because the
objectives were such a long way off and when the season did
finally start swimmers and coaches were reluctant to give too
much too soon; so instead of having a couple of noteworthy
swims each year many just dissipated their energy slowly
over the six-month competitive period. This has all been
changed now and we have a two-peak year, so that there is
never very long between each season and interest can be
more easily stimulated. For twelve months before the 1970
Commonwealth Games I spent a considerable amount of time
feeding information about the opposition to all of the 'possible'
Welsh team members. This helped them to battle through
their training because they were constantly kept in touch with
the reality of their work – success in Edinburgh. Scotland,
under their coach, Hammy Smith, worked with the same sense
of purpose.

If the science of swimming is applied by the coach in such
a way that it encourages the swimmer to work harder and
create within the individual a deeper interest in training and

competition then the psychology will have been successful. We find that swimmers, along with anybody else, improve in leaps and bounds. It is very rare to see a steady improvement curve; instead, improvements are followed by plateaux where nothing seems to get better. During these plateau periods the swimmer needs encouragement and variety to keep him going, and this can be supplied only by a coach who has a flair for applying his scientific knowledge to people.

8   Land Conditioning

Time is against the modern competitive swimmer: up to four hours, swimming a day and the coach is demanding that land conditioning be included in the programme! Muscular strength and shoulder and ankle mobility are two important attributes in swimming and can be improved very quickly by a series of land-based exercises. Circuit training can increase muscular and cardiovascular endurance, but as this is achieved more efficiently in the water it is rarely used, except as a welcome change from swimming. This chapter will be concerned with the development of strength and mobility rather than endurance, because I believe that circuit training cannot take the place of swimming training; it therefore plays no part in my swimming programme.

Strength Training

With the pressures of the limited time available, the coach will want to make sure that the land-conditioning programme is designed to derive as much transfer to the swimming situation as possible. The strength requirements of, say, a high jumper are completely different from those of the swimmer, so the training programme must cater for specific requirements. I will now trace my own search for specificity in the realms of strength training before moving on to the mobility exercises.

The consequences of strengthening a muscle are that it increases in size and weight; this means that any strength training must be designed to affect only those muscles which play an important role in propulsion. Extra weight and size merely adds to the body resistance, and if the wrong muscles are strengthened not only will the training be a waste of valuable time and effort but it will not add anything to the propulsive power of the body. A simple example would be a longdistance runner who embarks upon a programme to strengthen his upper body, thus adding to the weight he has to carry around with him. If he strengthens his legs instead, the increase in power may compensate for any weight increase, which would certainly be the case in a sprinter.

Having accepted that we should guard against unnecessary strength training we now ask the question: 'What are the prime movers in swimming?' This is not a very difficult question to answer because we have only to look at a good swimmer to see those muscle groups which are well developed. Muscles in the chest and arms provide most of the propulsion in swimming, but certain groups in the legs are used on starts and turns and breaststroke leg kick. A brief study of of any kinesiology manual[7] would soon give the reader a pretty clear idea of the muscles used in swimming propulsion. Opposite is a list of these muscles, most of which are prime movers, though the bottom two are really the link between the upper body and legs and require qualities of endurance rather than strength.

These groups of muscles can be strengthened through weight training, isometric exercises, pulleys, springs and minigyms. The real test of a particular type of exercise is whether there is an increase in swimming speed, though even when this does happen we do not really know the percentage effect of the exercises. It could be that improved technique is the reason for the improvement. In the final analysis we must find ways of strengthening a swimming movement by simulating it on land.

Latissimus dorsi *Pectoralis major* *Teres major* *Triceps* *Subscapularis*	Muscles of the upper body and arms which lever the body through the water
Flexor carpi onaris *Pulmaris longus*	Muscles which hold the wrist and hand in the water; they keep 'the paddle' rigid
Quadriceps *Gastrocnemius* *Gluteus maximus*	Muscles used in starts and turns and breaststroke leg kick
Rectus abdominus *Iliopsoas*	Trunk muscles which help to stabilize the movement of the upper and lower body

Weight Training

It is very easy to isolate the muscle groups, as above, and devise a series of specialized weight-training exercises to strengthen them, but whether they will then work together in an efficient manner is open to question. For instance, the 'bench press' exercise strengthens the *pectoralis major* and 'bent-over rowing' has the same effect in the *latissimus dorsi;* but while both of these muscles play a major part in swimming propulsion their newly acquired strength may not blend into the swimming movement. No attention has been paid to the timing of a complex movement which could well be altered by an increase in strength. Weight training can strengthen specific muscle groups but not specific movements. Accepting the disadvantages of weight training, I will outline a few exercises that can strengthen the prime movers.

Bench Press Lying on a bench with feet firmly on the floor (figure 34) to help him balance and the arms extended above

Figure 34

the face, the subject grips the barbell outside the shoulder width. The movement involves bending the elbows and allowing the barbell to come down to the chest and then back to the arms-extended position. From my own experience a wide grip puts a greater strain on the *pectoralis major*.

Muscles exercised: *pectoralis major*.

Bent-over Rowing Bend forward until the trunk is nearly at right angles to the legs and, where possible, rest the forehead against something firm (such as the top of a radiator or vaulting horse). With the feet apart and the arms extended below

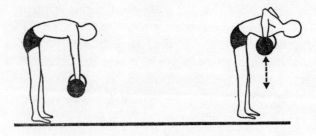

Figure 35

the body (figure 35) grip the barbell at shoulder width. The movement involves drawing the barbell up to the chest and back down to the arms-extended position.

Muscles exercised: *latissimus dorsi.*

Bent-arm Pullovers Lying on the back with the barbell just behind the head, grasp the bar, palm upwards with a wide grip (elbows bent at 90 degrees) (figure 36) and on the ground

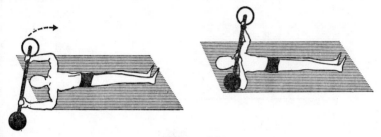

Figure 36

at shoulder level. Raise the bar in an arc to the vertical position above the face, keeping the elbows on the floor. Return to the start and do not arch the back.

Muscles exercised: *pectoralis major, subscapularis, latissimus dorsi, terres major.*

Straight-arm Pullovers Lying in the supine position on the floor grip the barbell with arms extended behind the head, palms upwards at shoulder width. Raise the bar in an arc to the vertical position above the face without bending the elbows and return to the starting position. The only difference between this and the last exercise is that the arms are kept straight.

Muscles exercised: *pectoralis major, latissimus dorsi, terres major, rectus abdominus.*

Sitting Bent-arm Pullover Sitting on a bench, the barbell is held behind the head with the hands gripping it, palms upwards and hands about twelve inches apart. Keeping the elbows close to the head (figure 37), the subject moves the

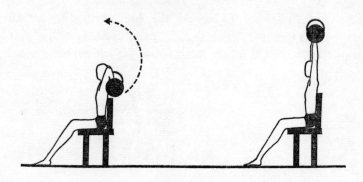

Figure 37

barbell to a position above the head where the arms are fully extended.

Muscles exercised: *triceps.*

Backward Arm Press Standing with the feet apart and knees bent (figure 38), let the bar rest on the fingers behind

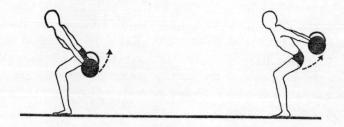

Figure 38

the body, palms upwards. Swing the bar upwards and backwards in an arc by extending the elbows. Care should be taken not to use the legs to help the movement.

Muscles exercised: *triceps, flexor carpi onaris, palmaris longus.*

Half Squats Standing with feet apart, the barbell resting across the shoulders and the hands gripping it to help balance, the subject bends his knees until a right angle is formed between the upper and lower leg (figure 39). He then returns

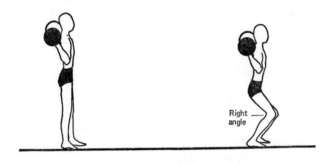

Figure 39

to the erect position and stands on his toes. Because of the great weight involved sound technique is important and the head must never be allowed to drop because the back will bend and the body can easily overbalance. There are some very sophisticated leg-exercising machines which are much safer to use because they take the weight off the shoulders.

Muscles exercised: *quadriceps, gluteus maximus, gastrocnemius.*

Full squat, where the seat moves down to the heels from the same erect position as mentioned above, is a good exercise

G

for breaststrokers as it attempts to strengthen the wider range of the leg kick.

Sit-Ups Lying on the back with feet either held or fixed under wall-bars and a weight held behind the head, raise the

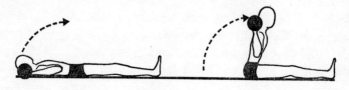

Figure 40

trunk to the vertical position (figure 40) and back down to the floor.

Muscles exercised: *rectus abdominus.*

Leg Raises Lying on the back with a weight attached to the feet and legs out straight, raise the feet about twelve inches from the ground and return to the start.

Muscles exercised: *iliopsoas.*

Many coaches will not agree that the last two exercises are important to swimmers. I would go along with them in that I would consider that they may require endurance rather than strength, but I believe that too many young swimmers find difficulty in maintaining full body rhythm because the abdominal muscles are weak. A few sit-ups and leg raises every day soon help to solve the problem.

If weight-training exercises are going to improve muscle strength the resistance and number of repetitions must be considered. My own personal preference for the number of repetitions for any exercise is six, but most authorities indicate that as many as ten repetitions will improve muscle strength. The swimmer and coach have the choice of doing anything from three to six sets of three to ten repetitions of a particular exercise. Because we know so little about muscle strengthening it seems reasonable to add variety to the training programme.

There is no formula that can be applied to the weight a swimmer should be using for each exercise because we all have differing amounts of natural strength. If an individual can bench press 150 pounds for six repetitions he is capable of handling a greater resistance over three repetitions. The principle of progressive resistance is applied to strength training because once an exercise becomes easy its effects diminish.

To derive the greatest benefit from any strength training the muscles should not be tired. I suggest that a swimmer should perform a hard weight training programme every other day, at a time when he is fresh. Before he starts the muscles should be warm to avoid any possibility of strain and it is advisable for swimmers to work in a group, since accidents can be avoided if they co-operate with one another in supporting heavy weights.

Working on the assumption that a swimmer can train three times a week here is a chart suggesting a way of using a variety of sets and repetitions with the objective of acquiring strength. This type of training can become very time-consuming and it is sensible to put a time limit between sets of repetitions, say two minutes, in order to cover all the work as quickly as possible. The order in which the exercises are done is also very important and where possible upper body exercises should be fitted in between other exercises so as to give the muscles a brief rest; the quality of the exercise will then be improved. This type of exercise is known as an isotonic movement because the muscles are allowed to contract.

Strength-Training Programme

EXERCISE	DAY 1	DAY 2	DAY 3
Bench press	3 sets of 10	4 sets of 6	4 sets of 3
Half squat	repetitions on	repetitions on	repetitions on
Bent-over rowing	all exercises	all exercises	all exercises
Sit-ups			
Bent-arm pullovers			
Leg raises			
Straight-arm pullovers			
Backward arm press			
Sitting bent-arm pullovers			

Pulleys, Springs and Exergencies

The use of heavy resistance exercises like weights certainly strengthens muscle groups but there may be very little carry-over into the actual swimming environment. Coaches have tried for many years to resolve the situation and have developed another form of strength training: the use of elaborate pulleys or springs and exergencies where the swimmer can simulate the swimming position (figure 41). The swimmer can lean forward or lie on a bench and pull the resistance, which in this case can be varied. Springs and exergencies are used in the same manner, their advantage being that they can be transported easily and the resistance to the pull can be altered. The disadvantage of all the methods mentioned so far is that they cannot change their resistance during a particular pull. Imagine the swimmer in figure 41 pulling a resistance of thirty pounds. At the beginning of a pull he can just about move the pulley rope but when his arms get into position (b) he finds that the exercise is very easy, because his body can incorporate more muscle action in this position; he will therefore not add any strength to this part of the movement. His ability to perform the exercise will be dictated by the resistance he can move in the first part of the pull so he will be strengthening only the first part of the movement. This does

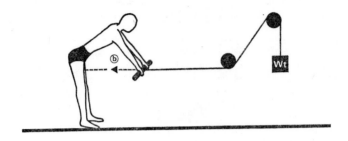

Figure 41

not mean that apparatus of this nature does not have some effect; it certainly does, but the search for more efficient means is going on. We cannot afford to be satisfied. As in exercises with weights, these methods are known as isotonic movements, but they have the added advantage of being performed in the swimming position.

Isometric Contractions

Isometric exercises allow groups of muscles to work maximally against an immovable object, but the muscles do not shorten and there is no limb movement, as in swimming or any other activity. Figure 42 illustrates a swimmer lying on a bench in the prone position. He exerts a maximum force against the static object O in position A; then the object is moved to position B and C and so on, and the swimmer exerts pressure in these positions throughout the range of movement of the swimming stroke. Evidence suggests that the muscles are certainly strengthened in these differing positions, but nobody can say conclusively whether the whole movement is made more efficient.

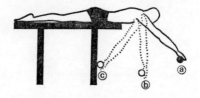

Figure 42

Up until 1969 many coaches combined weight training, pulley and chord work with isometric exercises in the hope that the results would be a stronger complete movement. Research by American physical therapists resulted in the mass-production of a new machine called the 'mini-gym', the first of which arrived in Britain in the autumn of 1970.

Mini-Gym

Once again, I feel that maximum transfer of training from land conditioning to the water will take place if a swimmer can simulate, as near as possible, his swimming pattern of movement on land. Councilman[3] reported that when the arm is pulled through the water the muscles, especially in an all-out sprint, do work maximally at every point in the pull and do not work against a constant force. In other words, the power of the arm pull changes throughout the movement. Take the case of a swimmer who finds that on the first third of a typical frontcrawl arm pull he can exert a maximum force of 50 pounds, on the second third 40 pounds and on the final third 60 pounds. Using pulleys or springs he would be able to exercise through the whole range of movement only by using a resistance equal to, or less than, the muscle power in the weakest part of the pull (middle third, 40 pounds).

From this example it can be seen that in weight training the total amount of weight a person can lift is that which his muscles can handle at the weakest point in their range of movement. Many swimmers overcome this problem in training with weights by speeding up the exercise movements at their strongest points, hoping that the momentum gained can help the muscles push the weight through the weaker points. A jerky and poor strengthening movement is thus created.

It was shown earlier in this chapter how isometric exercises allowed only for static and not dynamic strengthening, although the limbs are able to work against a variety of resistances in different positions of the pull. When a swimmer pulls his arm through the water the lever system changes and the arm is capable of creating greater force at certain points in the pull. This is known as isokinetic movement. It combines the varying force of isometric exercises with the movement of limbs and muscles in isotonic exercises. If muscles work isokinetically it seems only natural to exercise them isokinetically when performing strength-building exercises. The mini-gym is a small and extremely portable piece of apparatus and its advantages over other resistance apparatus are now accepted by all those who have had cause to use it in a variety of sports. Exercises which require very little apparatus and can incorporate the swimming movements are very easy and quick to perform. All the muscles mentioned in this chapter can be exercised in a few minutes instead of the hour or longer that is needed for weights. The work can be done at home, or just before training if the apparatus is set up at the pool. The best effects will be derived if the swimmer is not already tired and is warmed up.

The mini-gym is the latest piece of apparatus on the market resulting from the search for specificity, but it will probably be superseded by more sophisticated machines. Until such a time we must use the best methods available. In 1967 exergencies were introduced into Britain, but how many swimmers and coaches took the work on the machines seriously? Far too many people 'played at' strength training instead of taking the work seriously and exploiting the opportunity fully. Machines can now simulate the resistance throughout a limb movement; the next stage will be to simulate the speed at which the limb moves.

Mobility

We have already seen how time-consuming a strength training programme can become, especially if it is wasted on unnecessary exercises. Most swimmers have more than average flexibility of the shoulders and ankles, which is an asset in the sport. Previous chapters dealing with the four recognized strokes illustrated the importance of specific mobility, so there is no need to go over the same ground again. The performance of a particular stroke can maintain and improve the level of an individual's mobility but, once again, land-based exercises can do the same job more efficiently. The ideal time to do these exercises is after a session of strength training because there is a real danger that muscles could lose some of their flexibility. As the swimmer reaches early adulthood he becomes aware of a tightening of the muscles round the joints; if he does not adhere to a flexibility programme he is in grave danger of losing an important attribute, especially if he is very muscular. Girls are generally much more flexible than their male counterparts, so exercises may not be so important for them.

If pressure is suddenly applied to a muscle to make it stretch it reacts to prevent the movement taking place so that it will not be overstretched. The easier way to improve mobility is to apply a steady force on the muscle, thus stopping the reflex action. This force can be applied to the subject either by a partner or by the subject himself. The following exercises are designed to increase the range of movement of shoulders, ankles, hips and knee joints and should be performed about forty times steadily (squeezing movement), avoiding jerks which could set up a reaction to the movement within the muscle.

Shoulder Mobility   1 The subject (S) (figure 43) places his hands behind his back, keeping his arms straight and body

Figure 43

erect. Partner (P) holds his wrists and moves the hands and arms upwards as far as they will go. By moving the hands apart he can lift the arms higher and then perform a movement of squeezing the subject's hands together.

2 The subject grasps a piece of rope or a bar over his head

(figure 44) and keeping his arms straight and his hands as close together as possible moves his arms backwards over his

Figure 44

head (figure 44b). The advantage of this exercise is that improvement can be measured as the hands come closer together on the rope or bar.

Ankle Mobility 1 Sitting on the floor with legs extended (figure 45) the subject's toes can be pressed by a partner

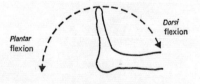

Figure 45

in either of the two directions shown in the diagram. *Dorsi* flexion is a useful exercise for breaststrokers whereas *plantar* flexion improves ankle flexibility for the kicks used in the other three recognized strokes.

2 The subject kneels on the floor with toes extended behind him; he sits back on his heels and then raises his knees off the ground, putting his weight on the top of the foot and maintaining balance by keeping his hands on the floor behind the body. This improves *plantar* flexion.

Hip, Knee and Ankle Mobility The subject kneels on the floor with the toes turned out to the side as in a breaststroke leg kick. With the hands supporting him behind the body, he sits back on the heels. Once he has mastered this position with his body supported by the insides of the foot he can lift his knees off the floor and rock back on his heels. I find that this position is good for breaststrokers, although many take a long time to master the movement.

There are numerous exercises that coaches have devised to improve mobility but I have given only a few because I feel that time can be wasted by going through too many movements. The reader may perform other exercises, but as long as they are objective and not time-consuming the effect will be the same or even better. To offset boredom it is sometimes a good idea to perform a series of exercises for a month and then compare their effect with a different set of movements the following month. An improvement in mobility is required only by those swimmers who find that their swimming strokes are being severely restricted; the others need only maintain an already sufficient degree of flexibility and the time they save by not attempting more exercises can be utilized in other areas of swimming training.

Specific land-conditioning programmes can be of immense practical value to the individual swimmer, but I believe that, but for very rare occasions, it should never become a substitute for water work. In 1968 the British Olympic 'possibles' had a number of training weekends at the Crystal Palace National Sports Centre. The highlight of the weekend for many of the men was the five-a-side soccer match, when coaches and swimmers embarked upon a high-spirited display of physical violence and verbal destruction. As a land-conditioning activity it was of no possible physiological benefit but as a change of activity it was a welcome interlude. A coach who has a finger on the 'pulse' of his squad will know when to use land conditioning for psychological or physiological reasons.

9 Planning the Year

The prospect of four hours' swimming training and, on top of that, a land-conditioning programme every day is not attractive to youngsters unless they are achieving some measurable success in the sport. Pressures are very real in modern swimming and it is becoming harder to achieve success unless the individual is the product of a system based on realistic planning and organization. Coaches throughout the world plan the competitive years meticulously. They select one or two competitions each year, normally the national championships, when they demand peak performance from their swimmers. As we have seen, in 1971 Britain adopted the 'two-season' year with short-course championships round the Easter holidays and the long-course championships in August. No longer do British swimmers have a twelve-month build-up to major competition and I am sure that coaches are finding it much easier to motivate their swimmers. The problems of planning for the Olympic Games, which normally fall in October, will not be dealt with directly in this chapter but it is hoped that the swimmer or coach can adjust any yearly plan to suit specific requirements.

It is highly unlikely that continued success will come from a centre which does not boast the following organization:

Coach + facility + swimmers + competition = success.

Lose any part of the formula and the success element will be very low indeed. Later chapters will deal with the role of coach and swimmers and on the question of facility it has already been shown how much daily swimming time is required. There are still many competitive set-ups in Britain that cannot comply with the conditions mentioned above and must rely upon crash weekend or one-week courses to provide a background of work just before the national championships. Months of hard work cannot be pushed into a week's intensive course and however much swimmers may abhor the idea of hours of daily training it is the only way of improving performance. I should like to see a time when twenty minutes' daily training will be the most efficient method of producing fast swimmers, but at the moment coach and swimmer have to accept the present gruelling conditions for success.

What, then, is the objective of a highly planned training programme? It is to produce a given time on a given occasion. The time produced will either place a swimmer first in the event or will be a satisfactory personal best performance. The objective must be realistic in that it can be achieved through hard work during the months of preparation and a 'cool head' during the crucial race. I have lost count of the number of times that I have seen swimmers break a record during the heats and then fail to repeat the effort in the final, thereby losing the race. Wendy Burrell, for instance, broke the European 200-metres backstroke record in the heats of the 1970 European championships in Barcelona yet was unable to win a medal in the final. This kind of situation will be fully reviewed in the next chapter, but it does illustrate the problem of realizing the year's work in a particular event.

The easiest way for me to show my ideas of planning a year's training is to imagine a group of thirty swimmers over the age of fourteen who are the basis of a team to win both team and individual titles in the national championships, both long- and short-course. There is an equal number of boys and girls and their specific targets divide them in the following manner:

200, 400 metres individual medley	2 boys, 2 girls
100, 200 metres butterfly	2 boys, 2 girls

100, 200 metres backcrawl	2 boys, 2 girls
100, 200 metres breaststroke	3 boys, 3 girls
100, 200 metres freestyle	3 boys, 3 girls
400, 800/1500 metres freestyle	3 boys, 3 girls

Obviously, this would be an ideal situation, but even in the normal club set-up it is a good idea for coach and swimmers to discuss their primary and secondary events for a given competition and train accordingly. For example, in 1970 Gary Hall was world record holder on 400-metres individual medley and 200-metres butterfly while Mark Spitz was in a similar position on 100-metres butterfly and freestyle; I am sure that they both had a particular event as their prime target and were also determined to exploit their talent fully in other events if at all possible. Similarly, Martyn Woodroffe's favourite event was the 200-metres butterfly, yet although success in this event was the basis of most of his training he did not neglect his medley and freestyle events, where indeed he established many British records. All these examples only go to show that the planning of a programme should have as an aim the development of individual talents.

Grouping

We have dealt with specificity in land conditioning and the idea is now accepted in swimming training as well, although there are coaches achieving success by giving all swimmers, regardless of the distance of their events, the same training programmes throughout the year. As in most other activities swimming success is relative; whereas general training may achieve faster times in age-group and district competitions it rarely achieves success in terms of world standards. The time may even come when specific coaches take, say, medley or breaststroke swimmers in a particular club, with an overall director to co-ordinate the efforts of the individuals into a cohesive team. This sort of picture seems to be emerging from East Germany, which is the second most powerful swimming nation in the world, although the organization is on a national rather than a club basis. To accommodate the variety of strokes and distances I, like many other coaches, divide the swimmers into three separate groups, always leaving room for swimmers to change if conditions warrant it. The breakdown is as follows:

SPRINTERS	MIDDLE DISTANCE	DISTANCE
100 m butterfly	200 m butterfly	400 m freestyle
100 m backcrawl	200 m backcrawl	800/1500 m freestyle
100 m breaststroke	200 m breaststroke	
100 m freestyle	200 m freestyle	400 m individual medley
	200 m individual medley	

At first glance, this would appear to be a very rigid breakdown, but one must accept that most sprint freestylers are also 200-metre swimmers and that, depending on the particular group, a coach may organize things differently.

If we go back to the stroke and distance breakdown of the imaginary group it will be seen that all the sprinters perform the 200-metre distance as well, so the organization in a six-lane pool may well be:

	SPRINT/MIDDLE DISTANCE			
	lane 1	lane 2	lane 3	lane 4
Distance	100/200 m	100/200 m	100/200 m	100/200 m
Stroke	freestyle	backcrawl	breaststroke	butterfly
Number	6	4	4	4

	MIDDLE DISTANCE/DISTANCE	
	lane 5	lane 6
Distance	200/400 m	400/800/1500 m
Stroke	individual	freestyle
Number	4	6

Any organization should be flexible and should never become the only way of arranging work-outs. For instance, better results may be gained from putting the men backcrawl swimmers with the women freestyle sprinters, because their repetition times may be similar and thus more incentive will be added to training. Lane 1 may well be classed as the sprint group, lanes 2–4 or 5 as the middle-distance group and lane 6 and possibly lane 5 as the distance group. The swimmers in lanes 1–4 will be concerned about sheer speed in their sprint event and pace in their 200-metre swim whereas those in lanes 5 and 6 will be more concerned with pace and endurance. An individual medley swimmer in lane 5 may be having considerable difficulty in settling down to a particular pace during a certain period of the year; he may well find that a few sessions with the sprinters improve his speed and he can then go back to his normal group, where he slips easily into his target pace. If the coach accepts that there is a difference in training for sprint and distance events he will produce a grouping arrangement to suit each swimmer's requirements.

As a prelude to the 1970 Commonwealth Games the Welsh team had a training camp at Aberystwyth University and amongst the group were two female and one male swimmer competing in distance events. They worked on a separate schedule but occasionally middle-distance swimmers did all or part of their sessions when we felt that it would be to their advantage. The overlap is always there but how much it is used will depend greatly upon the response of the swimmers to their normal work, which is designed to achieve a particular target. Those coaches who can see their swimmers only three times a week will find it an almost impossible task to plan a year's work comprehensively because they take part only in a small sector of a swimmer's training.

Assuming that the organization is sound and sympathetic,

H

what work should the swimmers do and when should they do it?

The Year's Plan

The two-season year has come to stay in Britain, so the short-course championship will be either at the end of March or in early April while the long-course nationals will come at the beginning of August. Each season can therefore be divided into three separate parts, each running into the other, and acting as a gradual build-up to the competition itself.

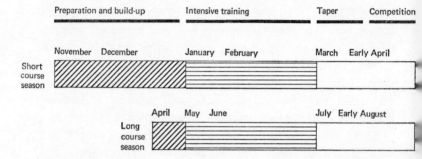

Short-Course Season It appears to be impractical in Britain to start intensive training in December as they do in America because those controlling facilities and coaching are reluctant to forego the Christmas festivities. There is, however, a growing awareness that unless British swimming is prepared to put itself out at this time of year, our results will always be behind the rest of the world. March is the critical month, because the coach has to decide when he is going to ease up the work and start tapering the swimmers.

Long-Course Season As soon as the short-course competitions have finished, the swimmers have a few days' rest and then begin a short build-up into another intensive period of work. For many swimmers, May and June are big examination months and I suspect that we would obtain both better swimming and better academic results if the long-course championships took place at the end of August, thus allowing more time for the hard core of work. July, like March, is a critical month and will be discussed fully in due course.

September/October A well-organized two-season year should leave the swimmer these two months when he is free to pursue other activities, such as water-polo, or something which gives him a rest from swimming activities. The Olympic and European Games make September and October periods of hard work for the chosen few, but the majority can take a well-earned rest, coaches and administrators included. But the longer a swimmer stays out of the water, the harder it becomes to achieve his previous high fitness level, so I would advise that some sort of swimming should be done during this phase. This period is the ideal opportunity to embark upon a strength-training programme because the body will not have to cope with the effects of daily training and there could well be rapid improvement during the two-month period. Although swimmers may want a rest at this time of the year, they have the thought at the back of their minds that they will lose too much of their hard-earned fitness; a land-conditioning programme or some other positive work will help allay such fears. To sum up this period, it is one of active rest.

Preparation and Build-Up (November, December, April) After a two-month lay-off from serious competitive swimming and training, November and December form the longer and harder of the two preparation and build-up periods. Correct stroke technique has to be re-established and starts and turns must be checked, as some swimmers can lose a great deal in two months. Others, especially young swimmers, come back with improved technique. I personally have never given a swimmer more than a month's lay-off and in many cases I have found that what had been lost by way of technique and fitness is more than compensated for by the swimmer's renewed vigour for training. The wise coach will exploit this renewed flair and set out a programme which will achieve the objective of swimming fitness as quickly as possible. By this I mean a state of being where it is safe both mentally and physically to push a swimmer into the period of intensive training. Throughout any of the phases of training I like to give one day off from work-outs each week, normally Saturday. During the first two weeks of preparation I expect swimmers to attend for a two-hour session on five days of the week, and then for the next three weeks for six days. To allow for an easy progression into the intensive work period I expect them to attend for six two-hour sessions and three early-morning work-outs, any alternate days of the week. The April period allows for a week's rest from swimming, followed by a rapid build-up over the remaining three weeks. The method in which this preparatory period is organized will depend solely on when Easter and the short-course championships fall. If they come in the middle of April the preparation period will fade and merge with that of intensive work, which allows for a couple of week's easy swimming. Assuming that Easter falls at the end of March, the reader may find the following chart of some help.

Preparatory period (number of daily work-outs)

MONTH	OCTOBER				NOVEMBER				APRIL			
Week	1	2	3	4	1	2	3	4	1	2	3	4
Mon	1	1	1	1	1	2	2	2	−	1	1	2
Tues	1	1	1	1	1	1	1	1	−	1	2	1
Wed	1	1	1	1	1	2	2	2	−	1	1	2
Thurs	1	1	1	1	1	1	1	1	−	1	2	1
Fri	1	1	1	1	1	2	2	2	−	1	1	2
Sat	−	−	−	−	−	−	−	−	−	−	−	−
Sun	−	−	1	1	1	1	1	1	−	−	1	1
Total	5	5	6	6	6	9	9	9	−	5	8	9

Stroke and Turning Technique

Improved techniques are 'grooved' into a swimmer by constant practice and the preparation of the year in a sensible time
to make any changes, because the swimmer will then have a
few months to accept the new ideas. I believe that most
coaches agree that this time of year is the best for making
technical innovations, though one can still see British swimmers
frantically trying to change their strokes literally days before
the national championships. Maybe this is a panic measure,
but the results are nearly always disastrous because the changes
cannot be fully accepted by the body in time. To completely
isolate stroke technique work from the 'daily slog' is also
courting future disaster, since the object of these sessions is
to change a swimmer's method of propulsion once and for all:
he must not be allowed to revert to his old methods from that
day onwards.

I remember discussing turns with a group of backcrawl
swimmers who were finding great difficulty in performing them
quickly. They told me that they had worked hard in special
sessions devoted to the technique of backcrawl turning but the
weakness in the system was that the coach did not actively
encourage them to use their newly acquired skills on every

backcrawl turn in training. Providing a theme for each training session is a favourite method of mine, and I like to devote the first fifteen minutes to short swims dealing with a particular part of all strokes, or of one stroke. A few one-length swims concentrating on body position with the coach correcting faults is then followed by a normal training session with the swimmers working hard to maintain their new body positions for the duration of the gruelling work-out. There is a danger at this time of year that coaches will allow bad habits to become established by being too concerned with the development of basic swimming fitness; technique and fitness are complementary.

Besides developing the techniques a swimmer would be wise to work hard on a strengthening programme because his newly acquired skills may rely heavily on stronger muscles. It is no use trying to lengthen a butterfly swimmer's pull if he lacks the strength to perform the movement. The swimmer must now be put in a situation where he can develop the endurance to perform the improved techniques over a long distance or at a fast pace. Over-distance swimming is a popular type of work-out at this time of year but I am rather sceptical because it is so easy to drop into a very slow stroke that bears little or no resemblance to the method of propulsion used in competition. A girl who is capable of 80 seconds for the 100-metres breaststroke would be wasting her time doing 200-metre swims in four minutes, since the pace is far too slow. I believe that any pace less than 75 per cent of competitive speed is not really adding much to a conditioning programme. Most of the work covered should be at 80 per cent speed which, referring back to chapter 6, will improve cardiovascular endurance and capillarization of the propulsive muscles; kicking or pulling work should also be performed at the same pace and over a variety of distances. I was once asked what percentage of the build-up period should be devoted to kicking and pulling practices and I answered that it all depends on the strengths and weaknesses of particular swimmers. A good approximation would be 20 per cent of the total work, but this could depend very much on the prevailing circumstances. Within the full stroke programme I insist that anything from 20 to 40 per cent of the distance covered should be of a medley variety, especially in the case of younger swimmers who have not really developed their latent talents. The diagram here illustrates the ideas that have been discussed so far.

The year's programme

Full Stroke		Kicking & Pulling	
40 per cent	60 per cent	40 per cent	60 per cent
Medley	No. 1 stroke	Medley	No. 1 stroke

There will be many occasions when sprinters, middle-distance and distance swimmers will work together on exactly the same programme, but because many sprinters would object to swimming repeat 500s it is not always wise to group them together. Using our imaginary squad, here is a typical two-hour work-out for this time of the year. The first five minutes of the session are devoted to an individual warm-up session by the swimmers and the following ten minutes consist of a series of one-length swims dealing with a technical point of stroke. This new point will now be applied in the following work-out:

Sprinters: (lanes 1-6)
10 × 100 m	no. 1 stroke	every 3 minutes
10 × 100 m	kicking	every 3 minutes
20 × 50 m	no. 1 stroke	every 1½ minutes
10 × 50 m	no. 1 stroke	every 45 seconds
10 × 200 m	no. 1 stroke	every 1 minute

Total: 5,500 metres

The resting intervals will vary considerably according to the stroke and the sex of the swimmer. For instance, a girl breast-stroker may not be able to repeat the 200-metre swims in under three minutes, so the resting interval would be changed for her. Ideally, the swimmers should be grouped in such a way that their resting intervals are all the same (say, male back-crawlers with female freestylers) and the amount of time spent swimming will then be the same. It is of course inconceivable that the breaststroker should cover the same distance as the freestyler in the same time. Suffice it to say that during the two-hour period the swimmers should be working for about 70–80 per cent of the time and resting for the other 20 per cent. There are sprinters who would find this type of programme too hard or too boring and the coach will have to meet them halfway to devise ways and means of sparking off their response.

Middle distance: (lane 7)

10 × 400 m	individual medley	every 6 minutes
5 × 100 m	kicking	every 3 minutes
10 × 200 m	no. 1 stroke	every 3 minutes

Once more, the rests can easily be altered to give a good ratio of work over rest and the kicking session will cater for individual requirements. For instance, there may well be a medley swimmer who is trying to improve his breaststroke, so all the legs-only practices will be performed on this stroke. The session can easily be tailored to the individual. Whenever a leg- or arms-only practice is used it should be done with as little use of artificial aids as possible, because these could alter the body position considerably. When I see swimmers lying across a large polystyrene float on a legs-only practice I always point out the error of their ways and tell them to move back down into the water. The same thing applies to those swimmers

who use floats for arms-only practice that lift their legs into
an unnatural position.

Distance: (lane 8)
20 × 400 m   no. I stroke   every 5½ minutes
Total: 8,000 metres

Distance swimmers do not always require the same percentage
of rest as sprint or even middle-distance groups because by the
very nature of their event they are often physically better
equipped for the endurance work. What is the point of allowing
a freestyler to go every 5½ minutes to repeat 400s and produce
a consistent time of 4 minutes 45 seconds (which would give
him a 45-second rest) if he could produce the same time going
every 5¼ minutes? The response from the swimmer must bear
a close resemblance to his level of fitness at that particular
moment and he should never be allowed to 'get off lightly'.

The danger in setting out an example is that it may be inter-
preted as the only way of achieving a particular objective.
If an objective is not being achieved, either the target is too
hard or the methods of approach are wrong. I know that if I
stuck rigidly to the grouping and type of sessions just mentioned I should not achieve the build-up objective of improved
technique, strength and cardiovascular endurance.

Intensive Training (January, February, March, May, June, July)

Local muscular endurance and speed or pace are the objectives
of these periods of training. The majority of swimmers will be
expected to attend for two two-hour sessions per day although
I have experienced success from the real sprinters by giving
them either three separate one-hour sessions or one two-hour
and two one-hour work-outs each day. This was especially

true during the last four weeks of intensive training when they were working for sheer speed and found that the one-hour sessions interspersed with good rests produced the most favourable results.

It is not always possible to arrange for three sessions per day but where possible I consider it to be worth while trying. At the Welsh team training camp sprinters and other swimmers who had very little history of hard work responded well to the one-hour sessions. The first practice at 6.00 a.m. was in the form of short-rest work designed to maintain the basic conditioning and was followed by the sprint session over 'fifties' and 'twenty-fives'. All middle-distance swimmers attended for sprints and it proved to be very popular. In the late afternoon, after a good rest, all groups came down to the pool for varying types of broken swims and 'race simulators'. The point I am trying to make once again is that although it is easy to set out a schedule to pressurize the endurance of the swimming muscles the swimmer may not respond unless the work appeals to him. A faster pace than the build-up period is required if there is to be any effect on muscular endurance and this can be done either by extending the resting interval or by shortening the distance to be swum.

Sprinters: personal warm-up

5 × 200 m	no. 1 stroke (broken at 50 m)	every 4 minutes
10 × 100 m	no. 1 stroke	every 3 minutes
20 × 50 m	legs only	every 1 minute
20 × 50 m	no. 1 stroke	every 1 minute

Total: 4,000 metres

This programme could be the basis of a two-hour session for sprinters, but it must be remembered that many are unable to tackle this amount of work if they try to produce 80–90 per cent of their maximum speed; the rests or amount of work can therefore be altered. Three one-hour sessions of 3,000 metres each may achieve the objective far more easily than two

two-hour sessions of 4,000 metres each. The first section of the
session is five 200-metre swims going every four minutes, with
anything from a five- to ten-second rest between each 50-metre
swim. Assuming that a freestyler's aim is to break two minutes
for the 200-metres, he can simulate the desired pace by taking
a short rest between each 50 metres. The rest is cut if he finds
it easy to maintain the desired speed.

Middle distance: personal warm-up

10 × 200 m	no. 1 stroke	every 4 minutes
10 × 50 m	no. 1 stroke, legs	every 1 minute
20 × 100 m	no. 1 stroke	every 3 minutes

Total: 4,500 metres

Medley swimmers may pursue most of the session on either
straight medley swims in the 200 metres; in the 20 x 100
metres they may well profit from doing 500 metres on each
stroke. The variations of stroke, rest and pace are unlimited
and should be used intelligently. This group would do another
work-out in the day of anything from 4,000 to 8,000 metres,
so pace would be related to the whole day's work.

The coach would expect the 400-metre swims to be faster than
those performed in a build-up period because the swimmer is
only doing half the amount of work; but this session has once
again to be seen as just a fraction of the work covered in this
period, so no sweeping statements about percentage increases
in time should be made. The swimmer may be attempting this
session on a Friday evening when he is really tired after a
heavy week's work and his times could be very poor indeed.
I believe, however, that a coach should counteract fatigue on
most occasions by offering a challenging programme.

Distance: personal warm-up

3 × 30 × 50 m	no. 1 stroke	every $5\frac{1}{2}$ minutes
10 × 400 m	no. 1 stroke	every 45 seconds

Total: 8,500 metres

The three sets of 50-metre repeats are aimed at the 1,500

metre swimmer who is attempting to hit a pace that he believes he could hold under racing conditions over this distance. The resting interval given will not necessarily suit both male and female swimmers and can be altered accordingly.

This period should produce quantities of good quality work and gradually bear closer resemblance to the races ahead. From the beginning of the build-up period the pressures on the swimmers have increased and the coach demands great effort to ensure that the maximum adaptation is taking place. Under this intense pressure efficient technique must be maintained; at the first signs of a breakdown remedial action should be taken, in the form of either longer rests between repetitions or a complete change of programme.

Taper

How and when to ease up on training to prepare a swimmer for a major event has been the subject of numerous papers, yet we are still nowhere nearer to laying down any rigid rules. Because individuals react so differently to training they require an individual taper, the only valid generalization being that sprinters require a longer taper than middle and distance swimmers. The following chapter will enlarge upon the taper and competition period, so the work-outs given here illustrate only a small fraction of the work covered during this period. Swimmers have to be given work which will maintain their endurance level and increase their speed, in the case of sprinters, and pace, in that of distance swimmers.

Sprinters: long warm-up – kicking and pulling

3–4 × 100 m	no. 1 stroke	every 10–15 minutes
10 × 50 m	no. 1 stroke	every 2–3 minutes

Sprinters can go too fast in a 100-metre race and 'blow up' quite easily. As an example, Zac Zorn led the field down the first 50 metres of the freestyle final in the Mexico Olympics and reliable sources told me that his first length was faster than he had ever swum before; yet he was easily overhauled in the homeward length. Unless the sprinter is in control of his stroke he will soon find the whole rhythm breaking down. In the typical work-out given above the swimmers work to produce three or four fast 100-metre swims. They may have instructions to hit a certain time on the first length and then find out whether they can still maintain enough speed to finish in a given time. The sessions are now simulating a few of the conditions encountered in a race.

Middle distance: personal warm-up

5 × 200 m no. 1 stroke, broken at 50 m	every 5–6 minutes
5 × 200 m no. 1 stroke, broken at 100 m, 150 m	every 6 minutes
10 × 50 m no. 1 stroke	every 2 minutes

After the warm-up period swimmers go through the first set of 200-metre swims and aim to hit a pace related to their competitive targets. For instance, a breaststroker may aim to break 2.35.0, which would mean a pace of around 38.5 seconds for each of the 50 metres. With a 10-second rest he finds the target easy to achieve. The second set of 200 metres are broken at the 100- and 150-metre distances; these breaks simulate the race more closely and if the rests are reduced to as little as three or five seconds the exercise can be made very tough indeed. In fact, the swimmer may complete only two or three of these swims before fatigue sets in, but the objective will already have been achieved. The 50-metre swims at the end of the session may well be done with the sprinters, either as light relief or as a serious stroke re-establishment section, depending on the mood of the group.

Distance: personal warm-up

3 × 30 × 50 m	no. 1 stroke	every 40–50 seconds
or		
10 × 8 × 50 m	no. 1 stroke	every 35–45 seconds

This is just one of the two sessions that the distance swimmers will do at the beginning of their taper. The 1,500-metre and 400-metre swimmers are given a choice of session and aim to hit a target time for the repeat 50 metres. A swimmer trying to achieve, say, 16.30.0 for the 1,500 metres will try to hit a time of about 33 seconds, while another swimmer may well do one straight 1,500-metre swim followed by five 400-metre swims, at the coach's direction. Towards the competitive period this group will drop down to one session a day if the coach is sure that conditioning will not be lost and that the swimmers require more rest.

Taper and race preparation are so much interwoven that I have set aside the next chapter to show the final preparations for 'the big day'. Throughout the year the swimmer will be subjected to the pressures of swimming for his club but he must not neglect his daily training in favour of the side issues. The ultimate objective must always be made to loom large in his mind and he should endeavour to programme his day to fit in studies, sleep and other activities.

Nothing has been said about the total daily mileage of the different swimmers. This is deliberate, because swimming training is a steady progression over the years. In 1968 Martyn Woodroffe could not conceive of any swimmer doing more than 8,000 metres of good work each day, yet the following year he could take more work and managed 10–12,000 metres per day. Adaptation is a continuous process if the stresses put upon the body are always changing. It is no use doing 20,000 metres daily during the intensive period if the swimmer is responding to only about half of the distance. Never do what others have reputedly done just for the sake of saying: 'I did what George Haines did.' It may be disastrous to your swimmers.

10 Race Preparation

As my knowledge and experience of competitive swimming have grown I have become more sceptical about the training methods I adopt. It is impossible to measure accurately the effects of particular types of training and what is learnt is therefore based very much on a subjective assessment. As long as this assessment is the result of observations on individuals rather than on a group then it will have some validity. Out of a team of twelve swimmers ten may do personal best performances in the national championships and this success can often eclipse the relative failure of the other two; yet the coach should reappraise the effects of his work upon these swimmers in the hope of finding the right formula for success in the future. Talking to the successful swimmers may reveal weaknesses which, when corrected, could result in even better performances next time round. For instance, a sprinter may admit that although he won the race his stroke broke down completely over the last 10 metres. Action can then be taken to avoid a recurrence in the future.

Taper and race preparation are similar to the tuning of a racing car, where all the preceding months of improvement of engine performance, aerodynamic shape and so on are useless if the car is not finely tuned. The only difference in swimming is that the driver and vehicle are one and the same thing. Mind and body need tuning to make them work together in achieving an objective that they believe to be within their capabilities. Throughout the months of preparation the coach may say to a swimmer that he is capable of doing 69.0 seconds for the 100-metres breaststroke, but whether the swimmer is really convinced is entirely up to the coach's powers of persuasion; people are convinced by being shown rather than told that a particular task is possible. The exceptions to this rule are those who have an inherent faith in their own ability to conquer despite the odds, but this faith comes only from experience in similar circumstances. Before Neil Armstrong nobody from earth had ever landed on the moon, yet the captain and crew took the chance because they had tested all the equipment beforehand and had sufficient faith that it would all function in the unexplored environment. The swimmer's equipment must also be fully tested before he can be convinced that it will function efficiently under the stresses of a race.

The following example concerns an imaginary breaststroker who wants to do 69.0 seconds and 2.34.0 seconds for 100 metres and 200 metres respectively. There are four weeks to go to the national championships and the coach has to convince him that his work background is such as to produce these times on the day. One danger of writing down a taper programme is that it appears to be rigid, but the idea is simply that the coach should have this blueprint in his head, knowing that he may have to change it to suit daily conditions.

Week 4 This being the last week of intensive training the swimmer will work out twelve sessions and they may well take the following pattern:

Sunday	session 1	conditioning	session 2	sprints
Monday	session 1	sprints	session 2	broken swims
Tuesday	session 1	conditioning	session 2	sprints
Wednesday	session 1	sprints	session 2	high-quality swims
Thursday	session 1	conditioning	session 2	sprints
Friday	session 1	conditioning	session 2	broken swims
Saturday	session 1	rest day		

Week 3   The number of sessions now drops down to nine for the week and the swimmer is encouraged to rest:

Sunday	session 1	conditioning	session 2	sprints
Monday	session 1	rest	session 2	broken swims
Tuesday	session 1	conditioning	session 2	sprints
Wednesday	session 1	rest	session 2	high-quality swims
Thursday	session 1	conditioning	session 2	sprints
Friday	session 1	rest	session 2	broken swims
Saturday	session 1	rest day		

Week 2   The sessions are now reduced to six per week so that the swimmer can take even more rest and derive greater benefit from each session. Late morning or early afternoon often produce the best times for one daily session because the swimmers seem to be alert, as long as they haven't gorged themselves with food.

Sunday	conditioning
Monday	sprint work
Tuesday	conditioning
Wednesday	broken swims
Thursday	conditioning/sprint work
Friday	broken swims
Saturday	rest day

Week 1   We will assume that the championships begin at the end of this week, although the whole work plan could easily be extended if they did not start until the following week.

Sunday	conditioning/sprint session
Monday	broken swims
Tuesday	sprint session
Wednesday	broken swims/sprint session
Thursday	travelling to venue
Friday	session of easy swimming to get used to competition pool
Saturday	day of first race

We will come back to this last week later on in the chapter, after an explanation of the type of material covered in the four-week period.

I

Conditioning

Distance swimmers rely heavily on cardiovascular conditioning for success in their races and, to a lesser degree, so do sprinters and middle-distance specialists. The type of work used to improve or maintain high levels of conditioning has been discussed in earlier chapters and it only remains to say that these sessions remain in the taper period as a safeguard against loss of conditioning. How many sessions of this work are needed by each group or individual per week will depend entirely upon the coach's previous knowledge and his ability to read the present situation of the swimmers. He may feel after discussion with the breaststroker at the end of week 3 that this individual requires more or less conditioning in the following week than the outline suggests. Much of his information will be derived from shrewd observation of the broken swims, sprint and high-quality sessions.

Sprint Sessions

To me these sessions mean fast work over distances of 25 and 50 metres where the swimmer is endeavouring to reproduce a certain time with relative economy of effort. We have already said that 'breaststroker Bill' wants to swim 100 metres in 69 seconds, which means that he will have to go through the first 50 metres of the race around 32.5–33.0 seconds, giving him a safety margin of 36 seconds on the second length to allow for the onset of fatigue. Bill will become very disheartened if he finds that it is a real struggle to sprint 32–3 seconds in training, because he knows that he will be far too shattered to do anywhere near 36 seconds on the home straight. The sprint work, then, must be designed to give Bill a chance of success.

Here is a typical session that I have used in a variety of forms on many occasions.

1	Long warm-up		
2	10 × 50 metres	no. 1 stroke	every 3 minutes
3	10 × 50 metres	no. 1 stroke, legs only	every 2 minutes
4	5 × 50 metres	no. 1 stroke	every 3 minutes
5	10 × 25 metres	no. 1 stroke	every 2 minutes

1 The swimmers are told in advance what the session will contain and the reason for doing certain work and are then advised to warm up and be in a state where the objectives can be achieved.

2 Bill has been told to hit 33 seconds in this part of the session, although he will probably not achieve the time until the third or fourth swim because he may find difficulty in getting his body to function at this pace. The time he takes to achieve a 'hot pace' will also give the coach an indication of the sort of pre-race warm-up he should do.

3 Legs-only offers a brief respite to the arms and upper body, yet it can be performed at a fast pace in order to help maintain local muscular endurance.

4 Before these 50-metre swims the coach may have a word with the swimmers about the lessons to be learnt from the previous set and inform them that as they are doing only five instead of ten they should be faster or else the target time should be achieved with ease.

5 A common fault among many sprinters is a general sluggishness over the first few metres of a race. 25-metre sprints can help to speed up the individual's reaction to the start of a race, especially his ability to settle into an efficient stroke quickly. I have known swimmers admit that they did not really find their stroke until the last 30 metres of a race, let alone after the first 20 metres.

Each part of the sprint session has a purpose and the

swimmers should be made fully aware of the objectives if they are going to give any real response. If Bill finds that he can hit 33 seconds with energy to spare then the work will have a convincing physiological and psychological effect.

Broken Swims

No coach in the history of swimming has been able to simulate the conditions of a race so as to find out how a swimmer will react. It is possible to simulate only a few of the pressures and very little can be done to gauge the effects that other competitors may have upon him. Broken swims, if they are well thought out, give both coach and swimmer an idea of what could happen in a race. Again we will take the case of Bill and imagine that we are back in week 4, the beginning of the period of transition from hard work to faith in his own ability.

Broken swims means that the racing distance will be broken down into shorter distances with short rests to enable Bill to maintain a racing pace. The 200-metre swims can be broken down into 4 parts of 50 metres each or 3 parts of 100 metres, 50 metres and 50 metres. Many other combinations are possible, but we will concern ourselves with the two examples mentioned:

1 The 200 metres are broken at 50 metres with a 10-second rest. Bill wants to do 2.34.0 for the 200-metre breaststroke, so that will mean maintaining a pace of 38.5 (2.34.0 ÷ 4) seconds. He should find this pace easy to maintain with a 10-second rest at the end of every 50 metres, even if he does 6–10 of these broken swims. They can be made tougher by reducing the resting interval to 5 or even 3 seconds; then Bill really begins to feel the pressure. But, to be realistic, no one ever swam a race using the same pace for every length! We

must, therefore, put everything into perspective because the longer the race lasts the more tired the swimmer will become, so he must have a strong pace for the first half of the race while he is still fresh. The pace for Bill's race could be 35.0, 38.5, 39.0, 41.5, in order to achieve a final time of 2.34.0. If we apply these times to the earlier examples the swim becomes a little more realistic.

2 The first half of a 200-metre race is relatively easy and the case for giving a rest at the completion of the first 50 metres of a broken swim can be questioned. It is more realistic to allow the swimmer to complete the first half of the race before giving him a rest; then in the second half he will find it harder to maintain his target time. Using this type of swim Bill would be allowed a 10-second rest at the 100- and 150-metre distances. If the target times are kept the same he would want to cover the first 100 metres in 1.13 (35 + 38.5 seconds), the 150 metres in 1.52.5 (1.13.5 + 39.0) and the 200 metres in 2.34.0 (1.52.5 + 41.5). With a rest as long as 10 seconds he may do this easily, but again a variety of rest intervals will change the pressures considerably.

During the four-week taper period the coach may set aside one session for each of the two examples every week or he may combine both types of work in each session. Whatever the method adopted the swimmer should achieve the end result; care must be taken not to do this or any other quality work if he is showing signs of fatigue, since failure can play heavily on his psyche.

The same principles can be adopted for any distance or any type of event because the aim is to encourage the swimmer to do as much work at racing speed as possible.

Readers may note that each week of the taper the swimmer does less work and is encouraged to take more rest both in and out of the water. Ideally, Bill should be able to hit his

target times on broken swims in week 4 with 10 seconds'
rest and the final week with 3 or 5 seconds' rest. As he does
less work the quality increases and the mental and physical
taper should be reaching a peak. The following examples show
the weekly build-up with broken-type swims:

Week 4
5 × 200 (broken at 50 m with 10 seconds)	every 6 minutes
3 × 200 (broken at 100 m and 150 m with 10 seconds)	every 7 minutes
Target: 2.34.0	

Week 3
3 × 200 (broken at 50 m with 5 seconds)	every 6 minutes
3 × 200 (broken at 100 m and 150 m with 5 and 10 seconds)	every 7 minutes

Week 2
The same as week 3 but with 3 seconds' rest if at all possible.
Week 1
The same as week 2, though it may well be advisable to do a
few more of the second type of broken 200s if the swimmer is
still not fully convinced. He may be frightened of the pain
he experienced; a few more during the week should dispel this
fear once and for all.

High-Quality Swims

An all-out swim over the racing distance returning a time of
anything from 90 per cent upwards of the required performance. A sprinter would be expected to return a 95 per
cent and upwards effort, which for Bill would mean 72.5
seconds (69 + 3.5 − 10 per cent) for the 100 metres. The
swimmer cannot repeat many such swims (2 or 3 may be the
maximum), but if he can do a 95 per cent swim he should feel

elated and ready for any competition. A rest of anything from 10 to 20 minutes is given between each swim to ensure a complete recovery. In this type of work-out I always give the swimmer a special point to aim for; in Bill's case I would ask him to go out in the target time for 33 seconds and then see how well he comes back. This will help him to get used to the racing pace; he will know when fatigue sets in and with the right approach will learn to fight through this phase.

There is often reluctance on the part of swimmer and coach to do much high-quality work, but this is really evading the vital issue of putting the year's training to the test. How on earth can a swimmer be convinced if he has no experience of the situation? I still meet British swimmers who hope rather than plan for a particular performance; they are often disappointed. Imagine Bill experiencing pain as soon as he turns after 50 metres; unless he has faced similar conditions before he will play safe and slow down in case he 'blows up'. High-quality swims can be performed over the distance, but the longer the race the harder it becomes to produce anything above a 95 per cent swim. A typical high-quality session the week before the championships may well run as follows:

Personal warm-up

Sprinters	Middle distance	Distance
4 × 50 m No. 1, 3 mins	1 × 400 m	1–3 × 400 m No. 1,
2/3 × 100 m No. 1,	and/or	15/20 mins
10/20 mins	3 × 200 m No. 1,	
	15/20 mins	

All the groups may prefer to take part in the 50-metre sprints because this may help to put them in the right frame of mind. Where possible, the coach should work the swimmers in separate waves rather than putting them all through the swims at once. The feeling of being in the lane by himself often enhances a swimmer's performance, especially if the groups are swimming against one another, although too much internal competition can sometimes upset the form of certain individuals. Arranging the group to produce target performances from each swimmer is very much the responsibility of the coach, who will pull out individuals from the session when he feels that they have achieved their target. If the swimmer is happy with his performance after two swims there is often no point in doing a third. He may well already be convinced.

Middle and Distance Swimmers

Three or four weeks' taper is certainly far too long for distance and many middle-distance swimmers. It can often be too long for a sprinter, since he sees the taper as a signal for worrying about the big race and turns into a bag of nerves. Hard work keeps him occupied and the fine balance between the effects of the work and those of a nervous rest period has to be maintained by the coach. We have mentioned before how important endurance is to the middle and distance swimmers; unless plenty of conditioning work is incorporated in the programme right up to the last three or four days the endurance level could fall and have disastrous consequences in a race. These two groups of swimmers are more concerned with pace than with their ability to sprint. A 400-metre swimmer who wants to break 4.20.0 is not really worried about doing 100 metres in 54 seconds; he is more concerned with working out a pace that he can maintain over the full distance. He may aim to take the first 100 metres in 61.0 seconds, then settle down to a pace of 66 seconds for the remaining 300 metres. Like the sprinter, he will be out to convince himself that the pace is possible; if he is finding difficulty he still has some time to solve the problem by either increasing the conditioning side of the programme or taking a rest to give his body time to replenish the stores of energy. The broken swims during the last four weeks will convince the coach and swimmer either to act on any glaring weaknesses or to continue a much slower taper than the one followed by the sprinters.

The middle-distance swimmers require both speed and pace so their taper will be longer than that of the distance swimmers but shorter than that of the sprinters. Medley swimmers, especially over 200 metres, need speed and endurance, but it is impossible for them to acquire maximum supplies of both qualities. The more time they spend on endurance training the more they neglect their sprint training and vice versa, but as long as they have a target time to work for they and the coach can decide on the necessary balance of the two qualities.

Rest

Whatever the number of training sessions allotted to the various groups, the time out of the water should be spent on taking things easy, especially during the last two weeks of the taper. The body must be given a sporting chance to recover completely from the stresses of the previous months if it is to respond to the challenge of the ensuing competition. By rest I do not mean that swimmers should lie in bed all day. After adequate sleep they can lead a normal sedentary life, interspersed with training sessions which are designed to see whether the rest is helping to bring them up to the boil. There is always a danger of putting on weight when swimmers are not in heavy training, but with a little care and daily check on the scales this should not create any serious problems. I have said nothing about diet because I have never encountered any serious problems here. I should consult an expert if such a case arose. The only advice I have given in the past is to eat a variety of foods in moderation, especially meat, fish, cheese, milk products and vegetables. I rely heavily on a swimmer's commonsense if he has any diet or weight problems and I should act as mediator between swimmer and doctor.

The Day of the Race

The first day of the championships is always the hardest, because if the swimmer has a poor start it may be difficult for him to recover in time to make amends. After a light breakfast he goes down to the pool to familiarize himself with the water and the atmosphere. I should encourage him to go in for an easy swim to check turns and lane markings and to use his racing lane if he knows which it is. 'It's just like the pool at home,' Martyn Woodroffe said to me when he first swam in the Mexico Olympic pool: the first hurdle had been overcome successfully. After some arm and leg work and a few one-length sprints the swimmer may want to get out, especially if the stroke is feeling good. Before lunch the coach can give his 'pep talk', which should be designed to instil confidence and a positive attitude. What and how much is said depends on the personalities of coach and swimmer; some swimmers may need reassuring whereas others are quite happy to be left alone. I admired Australian Don Talbot's approach to the individual pep-talk at the 1970 Commonwealth Games. During the pre-race warm-up he would take each swimmer involved in a race aside, talk to him and reassure him. Having spoken to some of the Australians, I know they had tremendous respect for their coach and this was reflected in their fine performance.

The morning session can be followed by a light lunch and a rest, but the swimmers should not be allowed to sleep too long or else the bodily organisms will slow down. A wise coach will weed out the very nervous individuals who cannot sleep and who let the prospect of the coming race play on their minds and upset their delicate state of equilibrium. Their minds should be kept occupied by subjects far removed from swimming until the time for the pre-race warm-up. The difference between 'rarin' to go' and a state of extreme nervous tension is a very fine one and only experience of similar situations can assist the coach in judging this. Unusual actions point to a swimmer's unbalanced state, which offers another example of why it is so important for a coach to know his swimmers properly so that he can spot the unusual and nip it in the bud. The swimmer should experience 'butter-flies' in his stomach if he is going to perform well, but if he feels violently sick the stresses have perhaps got out of hand.

Pre-race warm-ups are often chaotic affairs with too many swimmers using too little space at the same time. The chance of using one's racing lane is almost nil, but if the swimmer has familiarized himself with the lane in a previous session he will not worry now. A swimmer at national championship level, or for that matter at any level, should know what to do by way of an initial warm-up: mobility exercises on land and in the water to obtain maximum range of movement, followed by an easy swim to alert blood supply and other bodily functions. The race will not be a slow affair so, depending on the particular event, the swimmer will begin to do some short-distance swims at an ever-increasing pace. Distance swimmers may prefer to do a decreasing series of 100-metre swims (say, 10 × 100 metres every 3 minutes, reducing 70–60 seconds) while sprinters and middle-distance swimmers may prefer to work over 50 and 25 metres, again on a decreasing basis. Bill, who is swimming the 100-metres breaststroke, may do a series of 6 × 50 metres, starting at 40 seconds and reducing to 32 seconds. Whatever the content the warm-up should aim at making the swimmer move with ease and comfort at the racing speed. The level of competition will often determine the length of warm-up and I refer once more to Martyn Woodroffe. He was used to covering anything from 600 to 1,000 metres in pre-race warm-ups until the final of the Olympic 200-metres butterfly. The occasion was a great one: the chance of an Olympic medal, a lifetime's ambition. Three years of hard work was at stake and Martyn showed his feelings in the form of a very tense swimming stroke. To rid him of most of the physical and mental tension I extended his warm-up period to nearly 2,000 metres, until he and I were both satisfied that his stroke was flowing and smooth. I am convinced in the light of other experience that he would not have been able to swim the race of his life if he had not swum the tension out of his body beforehand.

Once the pre-arranged split time has been comfortably achieved the warm-up is at an end and the swimmer can finish off the session with a swim down followed by a change into a dry costume and warm clothing. If he is now fully convinced of the following points he should achieve his aims:

1 that he really wants to succeed
2 that the previous training was ideal
3 that the target time is possible
4 that his way is the only way to swim the race and that he will not be upset by the tactics of other competitors.

There are cases of coaches desiring success more than the swimmer, which is why point 1 is so crucial. If the swimmer does not really want to do it all the other points will become meaningless and the whole concept will disintegrate.

Shaving Down

Male swimmers, especially in America, are in the habit of shaving the hair from their arms and legs and even from their chest in the belief that the increased sensitivity they feel when swimming will enhance their performance. There is no scientific evidence that shaving increases performance but the results seem to justify the means. Care should be taken not to let swimmers shave down for all contests; they should do so merely for a couple of really big swims each year, so that this then becomes part of the build-up ritual.

Whatever the type of race preparation and taper adopted, providing that it stimulates the final performance it can be deemed partly successful. It is only partly successful because we have not yet found a foolproof way of ensuring that everybody reaches maximum performance at the same time. For the sake of the art of coaching, I hope we never do.

11 The Team Ideal

In team games like soccer and rugby great players cannot rely upon their individual skills to win a game. They realize their own limitations and seek the support of their fellow team members to pierce the opposition's defensive system. The coach of a soccer team is faced with the problem of co-ordinating the differing skills of eleven individuals in such a way that their talents can be blended and utilized for the benefit of the team. To do this successfully, the coach must understand the temperament as well as the skill level of his players. I am sure that international team managers of the calibre of Sir Alf Ramsey study the opposing team many weeks before an international fixture and work out in their own minds a 'blueprint for success'. They must then find the players who will have the mental and physical ability to work to the plan without becoming too stereotyped and losing their individual flair. There are some people who would argue that swimming is an individual sport and that its organization cannot bear any resemblance to the realm of team games. I do not agree. At the grass roots of the sport, the swimming clubs, we find that the progressive teams are involved in league swimming. A coach realizes that if his club is to stand any chance of success in this type of competition it must have a considerable number of good-quality swimmers. He cannot rely for success on a couple of star swimmers because the team that wins an inter-club contest is the one that chalks up the highest number of placings in all events rather than the odd couple of first places.

In 1969 Britain entered a men's and women's swimming team in the newly formed European league, thus strengthening the case for developing swimming as a team sport. The men's team were outclassed and demoted to the second division but the women 'showed the flag' and remained in the first division. This type of swimming exposes weaknesses in particular events and the wise coach or governing body at international level will react quickly and strengthen the weak events in the team. British coaches have had very little experience in developing strong teams capable of entering fierce competitions; too many of our international swimmers experience the realities of intense swimming for the first time when they swim for the national team. The great international swimmers of today, with few exceptions, are the product of an efficient club organization and intensely fierce internal competition, not of four hours' daily training. Training should be as much mental as physical preparation. Swimmers who graduate through fierce inter-club competition to the national team will be 'battle-hardened' and should be able to take the stresses of international competition in their stride. British swimming is not really committed to developing a system of club-oriented competition and training and I am convinced that this is why Britain is a third-rate swimming nation.[8]

I have already outlined the amount and type of daily training that competitive swimming requires, yet the majority of swimming clubs in Britain have only two or three sessions per week. They cannot, therefore, take responsibility for the development of their team and they rely heavily on coaches who seek out daily swimming facilities and develop their own squads. Many squads consist of swimmers from a number of clubs who work conscientiously under the coach all week and then disperse at the weekend and swim for their individual clubs. The weaknesses of this system are obvious: the coach never fulfils his ideals of training a team which can compete as one unit; his experience of team swimming is non-existent; the swimmer's loyalty is split between coach and club, since the coach trains him while the club provides him with the competition. Effort is therefore dissipated instead of concentrated. There are enlightened clubs in Britain which take full responsibility for appointing a coach to direct the daily development of the swimmers and see that all the hard work is fulfilled in strong competition. Sadly, they are few and far between and until more such organizations fighting to become 'top dog' emerge, Britain will never have depth in her international teams.

An ideal competitive swimming club would be coach-oriented, its objective being to provide its young swimmers with a progressive structure of training and competition, leading to full international honours for those who possess the physical ability and drive. I have seen organizations in America and Canada that function in this manner and for those who are still unconvinced the following example should help to make the picture clearer. Club X has a membership of one hundred competitive swimmers under the direction of a chief coach assisted by two staff coaches, who are responsible for the development of the club's raw talent and age-group programme. The chief coach works with the senior squad but sets out the objectives for the age-group swimming programme and takes a personal interest in the work of the youngsters because the future success of his club lies with them.

Age-Group Squad

A separate chapter has been devoted to some of the problems associated with age-group swimming, so to eliminate any overlap this paragraph is concerned only with the organization and content of work-outs of swimmers between the age of eight and fourteen years. The range of ability will be as wide as the age range and the assistants will have a daily two-hour session to cater for the swimmer's needs, with the over-riding objective of developing a group of swimmers who are technically proficient in all four strokes and in the relevant starts and turns, and who enjoy competition and training. It may well be that the under-tens train only twice a week, but any swimmer showing signs of considerable mental and physical maturity should be given a programme that is challenging. This is not an easy task for the assistant coaches to fulfil and the chief coach should endeavour to educate them in the best ways of achieving the objectives. Medley training for all swimmers can add variety to the work, besides encouraging youngsters to develop their latent talents. A ten-year-old backcrawler could blossom into a brilliant freestyler at sixteen, but only if he has the chance to explore the technicalities of the other strokes. The ulterior motive is that the club is building up reserves of youngsters who are multi-stroke experts so that when permutated into the various swimming events they can do incredible damage to the opposition. All four strokes are included in the competition programmes of swimming clubs and the neglect of butterfly or individual medley strokes in the formative years of club swimmers can have disastrous consequences.

The Senior Squad

Suffice it to say that we know what work this squad should be doing. At the lower end it may contain swimmers under fourteen if the coaches agree that they will respond to the tougher training. This group is the shop-window of the club and its success will reflect the internal organization and powers of motivation of the coach. To consider training as much as four hours a day the swimmers must be highly motivated by a person who can give a taste of the success which could be the result of the hard work. It may be that a short-term objective is to beat a particular club in a couple of weeks' time where the

K

competition is going to be tough and the result will depend on one or two key events. There will be swimmers who know that they have no chance of winning their races, but the coach may impress upon them the importance of taking second rather than third place, since the extra point gained may be the difference between over-all success or failure.

Like a football manager, the coach gives each swimmer a job to perform that he knows is realistic; the squad is thus imbued with a sense of purpose and training takes on a new meaning. The key event may be the men's 4 × 100 metres freestyle team race, where the team posing the main threat to our imaginary club is as good as, if not slightly better than, our four boys. A personal best performance from each swimmer will be the only way of winning and so the coach must know the best order in which to send the boys in order to achieve this result. John has a best time of 57.1 seconds; Kevin 56.6; George 58.2; Ronald 57.6 and the reserve swimmer, Fred, 58.5 seconds. On the face of it the total best times should not be affected whatever the order, but the coach knows that George finds it difficult to respond when he is behind in a race whereas John loves a fight. So he decides to send Kevin, the fastest swimmer, first, knowing that he will establish a lead for George to take over. Ronald will go third and John, who doesn't mind if he finds himself down in a race, will swim the final leg. Illness in any of the swimmers will require the coach to change the order to suit the temperament of each of the four new swimmers. Here we see the coach in his new role of psychologist, creating conditions that are most likely to exploit the individual's talent for the good of the team. Besides catering for first-string swimmers the far-sighted club will attempt to create similar conditions for the up-and-coming champions who need to be blooded in tight competition; this will reveal their response to the pressures entailed. This responsibility for training and competition is borne by the chief coach and I believe that such a person can do the job well only if he is in regular contact with his swimmers. Coaches who never experience this merging together of individuals into a united team effort miss the real meaning of competitive swimming.

The team ideal removes the clinical aspect of training and can, therefore, become a very emotional experience. I remember watching an interview on television between a holder of the Victoria Cross and an interviewer who was commenting upon his brave action. The soldier replied to the effect that he was put in a position where he was so emotionally charged that he could either run away or perform the act of bravery that he did. Similarly, when involving a team in a build-up for a particular competition the coach must know the pressures he can exert on each swimmer, because too much could cause some of them to run away rather than stay to fight.

Swimmers, like anyone else, want to identify themselves with something that can offer some sort of security and an opportunity to develop their talents, whatever they may be. Whoever is responsible for this must possess the skill to detect latent talent, however small, to release it and to set up the right environment to develop it. This objective cannot be achieved with everybody, but it should remain the ultimate target.

By the intelligent use of competition the coach can command respect and a positive response from swimmers, but what happens when a team is soundly thrashed by the opposition? If this occurs too frequently the swimmers will lose heart and perhaps even search round for another activity in which to express their talents. An occasional beating does no harm as it shows that the team is not invincible, but if the competition is consistently too powerful then a lower standard should be sought until the team is ready to compete on equal terms. The same principle applies to international competition. Every four years the Olympic Games becomes the focal point of world sport and I believe that any national sporting body intent on success should gear the four-year build-up of competition in such a way that the weaknesses in certain events are eliminated and a powerful international team developed. British swimming has very few swimmers of world standard and it is particularly weak in certain events such as the men's 1,500-metres freestyle. There is very little internal competition over this distance and the national champion also knows that his winning time is about a minute behind the champions of other countries. He therefore stands no chance of selection for international honours and so the event holds no interest to him. Yet numerous international meetings could be used to raise standards in that the best British swimmers in these weaker events could be selected to compete against non-British swimmers of similar or slightly better ability. This would instil a sense of purpose and give British swimmers considerable motivation to train harder. The international fixtures can thus be used to raise Britain's internal standards and not merely as an end in themselves. Swimmers certainly derive satisfaction from being able to compete with the opposition on equal terms.

Britain has as much natural sporting talent as other countries of the world yet she does not have the conviction needed to create a system for recognizing and developing this ability. East Germany regards her top sportsmen as ambassadors for their country and for communist ideals and has a very successful organization devoted to maintaining a very healthy sports development programme. When the standard of a particular sport is very high the competitors regard it as a great honour to represent their country in international competition. Yet I often detect an air of discontent among some of the senior British swimmers. I was once asked whether I believed that American swimmers held national representation in higher esteem than their British counterparts. Of course they did, because the road to an American national team is long and tough and there is therefore a real sense of achievement when swimmers finally make it.

Competition in training can help to raise the individual's standard of performance but even this aspect can be overplayed. A club may well have three or four butterfly swimmers who are fighting one another to represent their squad. Occasionally, it is sensible to swim them against one another for the whole or part of a session, but if this is done too often one swimmer may come out on top and destroy the others. Some swimmers have enough problems in competing at interclub level without adding to the stress in training. Swimmers will have to face up to a challenge from their peers in the squad-training programme if the club is to continue with its policy of producing numbers of swimmers in all events. The young up-and-coming swimmer is very keen to establish himself as a team member and he probably regards every training session as a personal race against his rivals. He may consider that being 'the tops' in a training session is the same as winning a race; this is a rather naïve form of reasoning but nevertheless one that can upset the form of senior swimmers, especially those whose place he is directly challenging. It could be argued that such pressure would keep everybody on their toes, but just how wrong this supposition is can be shown by the following example. A particular breaststroker was experiencing difficulty in improving his racing time although he was working very hard. His nearest rival was going through a period of sensational improvement: it did not seem to matter whether he trained or stayed in bed all day, since his training and race times were still falling. The youngster began to challenge the older swimmer both in training and in heated verbal exchanges between repetitions and even in the changing rooms. Before somebody was hurt the two swimmers were put in lanes well away from one another and the problem was solved for the time being in a 'two-string' match, in which the senior boy showed his superiority where it really mattered – in a race. Competition should be used to develop talent, not to destroy it.

Opponents of team training in Britain always bring up the same example to support their case: the only medals won by British swimmers in the Olympic Games of 1964 and 1968 were awarded to Bobby McGregor and Martyn Woodroffe, two swimmers who had never experienced daily squad training. I prefer to argue that we won only two medals because we were not team-conscious and that our two 'loners' might have reached even greater heights if they had been products of a team. Certainly British swimmers are not battle-hardened when they enter major competition where the pressures are far in excess of anything experienced in Britain. Psychological studies show that they are just as aggressive as their foreign rivals, but Britain lacks the club and national incentives to light the fire in the belly of these competitors. The creation of teams to encourage individuals of varying ability to play a positive part in their success is their only hope of salvation. Standing on the block just before the start of a race with all the associated nervousness is a harrowing and lonely experience even for the old stager, so the less able competitor may derive some comfort in knowing that he can take third place in the race and still help his team to conquer the opposition. How lonely and exposed he would feel if he belonged to no team and took third place; his performance would not have the same significance.

12 The Coach

Harry Braund[9] applied business management techniques to his definition of the role of the coach – to get results by identifying, developing and perfecting skills. The objective of the role is very simple, but because *homo sapiens* is a complex and temperamental machine the methods of approach can become very involved. To achieve the desired results the coach must be convinced that they are within the grasp of the swimmers and, more important, the swimmers must be as convinced as the coach. Before taking a closer look at the methods adopted by the coach in his endeavour to achieve results we must consider his personality. Are all coaches the same? Is there a stereotyped swimming coach?

One personality trait that looms large in all research into coach personality is that of dominance; perhaps this trait is a prerequisite of leadership. At first glance dominance conjures up the picture of a tyrannical dictator, but a little thought and consultation with a dictionary should put the mind at rest. To dominate does mean to rule but not necessarily in a haughty and overbearing manner; the many other traits of the coach's personality will determine how he uses this particular distinguishing feature. In my book, the coach should be a leader who can inspire others to become willing followers; since people can be led up or down, the leader should have worthy values. This is especially true when the followers become mature and can question their own motives and those of their leader. If coach and swimmer have different values, leadership cannot be re-established by a tyrannical approach on the part of the coach. Once the objectives have been mutually accepted the coach's job is to establish discipline in his swimmers. True discipline is self-discipline and this is easy to maintain if the

coach has motivated the individuals sufficiently to try to
achieve success. Lord Montgomery[10] described 'the superb
discipline of the army – a discipline that does not consist of
slavish obedience to orders, but is a looser, more rational
framework of control in which the soldier's independence can
flourish unhindered'. This type of framework should be established by the coach as an ideal situation in which he can best
express his ideas and expect a worthwhile response from the
swimmers.

The vast age range of swimmers is a real stumbling block to
establishing an over-all framework of self-discipline because
the younger element does not possess the mental maturity to
understand the ideals. Such swimmers need more guidance and
supervision until they show signs of maturity, by which time
they can be given more say and control over their destiny.
Once the swimmer starts a race he is on his own; nothing the
coach has said can help him now if he has not been given the
opportunity to develop self-reliance and faith in his own
ability. It is no use his having faith in the coach's ability because the coach cannot swim the race; he can only give advice
before and after. Even the poorest swimmer can admire the
technical ability of his coach, but if he is not persuaded to do
something about his own ability there will be no real improvement and little chance of achieving success.

Applying management techniques, the coach who is hell-
bent on seeking success must concentrate all his available
energy and resources in the right place to get the right results.

The first principle is to identify talent, a very important
function of the coach because he does not want to expend too
much energy on swimmers who will have neither the natural
ability nor the personal motivation to achieve even a low level
of success. He can identify talent only if he sets up an intro-
ductory session in his club, encouraging interested individuals

to apply their mental and physical attributes to the task of learning to swim recognized strokes. At this level one sees tremendous potential but, unfortunately, many talented swimmers are not really sold on the idea of competitive swimming as a means of expressing themselves. Where possible, the coach must use all his powers of persuasion and motivation and lay down a programme to stimulate this talent. This is not an easy task when he has to compete against the glamour sport of soccer, but I am sure that a response from the coach to the budding swimmer has a dramatic effect in more cases than is usually realized. Recruitment campaigns are of value only if the initial experience of the recruits is worthwhile, in which case they are more likely to come back for more and give the coach enough time to identify the talent. A successful club with a powerful 'shop-window' will find it easier to attract latent skill than an organization which does not appear to be successful at anything. After England won the World Cup in 1966 there was an upsurge and awakening of public interest in soccer that had not been bargained for. The power and consequences of success are not always understood, but the coach should always be asking himself why youngsters should be attracted to his club and if he cannot find a suitable reason he had better do something about it, and fast. East German researchers estimate that it takes one thousand competitive swimmers to produce an Olympic champion, but nobody has estimated how many swimmers must be attracted to a club to produce one competitive swimmer.

Once talent has been identified it must be developed. Here again the responsibility falls heavily on the shoulders of the chief coach and his assistants. He must ask himself what he means by talent and whether his answer is tangible enough to be developed. Swimming is all about competition and if the youngsters derive no 'kick' from competing against one another then they are going to be quickly disillusioned with training. I believe that in this development stage the coach should see that his underlings become technically proficient in all competitive strokes and then seek out the type of competition that will best suit his raw recruits. If they achieve success and enjoy racing they will develop self-inspired motivation to train harder and become even more successful. Here we see the coach establishing a framework of self-discipline by making the work stimulating and interesting and making sure that the swimmers never lose sight of their objective. He incites them to work hard by continually reminding them of their reasons for training and then offering advice on the most efficient methods of achieving maximum conditioning.

Perfecting swimmers, like perfecting anything in this world, is an impossible task, but that does not mean that we should never attempt to alter the status quo. The coach should now become sensitive to the weaknesses of his swimmers and he can perform this duty effectively only if he has a sound working relationship with his top squad. Regular discussions of training sessions are important, especially if the coach believes that a certain type of training should be having a specific effect on the swimmers. It is only by observing and questioning that he can note the real effects, and the swimmer who feels that he is being intelligently involved in his future will respond to this type of approach. A prototype aircraft like Concorde is filled with a large number of instruments to monitor the effects of stresses for the designers and, in the same way, the coach needs to know the effects of his work. He can measure them to a certain extent by noting any improvement in racing time, but by establishing close liaison he may be able to use better methods to create an even greater degree of improvement. The fact that we are all complex individuals means that coaches cannot treat everybody in the same way, even in training sessions designed to improve physiological conditioning, because the mind still controls many of the physical actions. The real danger is that the coach may pander too much to the individual's idiosyncrasies when he should be encouraging him to sink some of his identity into a united team effort.

Roger Falk[11] has said that ten years' experience could well mean one year's experience repeated ten times over. Successful coaches have to guard against an air of complacency because there is always somebody else ready to rise up and knock them off their throne. Methods that have brought success one year should be changed the following year in the interests of the search for improved performance. It may well be that last year's methods bring last year's results and one cannot be impressed by coaches who live in the past. The publication of scientific research has expanded exponentially since the turn of the century and this also appears to be true of research into swimming and its associated problems. Much of the work may well be irrelevant or inconclusive but the coach has the responsibility to search out information which can improve his coaching effectiveness. A new discovery may well mean a complete reversal of his thinking, but if he is convinced that it will bring increased success he must be strong enough to explain his change of approach to his swimmers. If they have faith in his ability they will look forward to an even more successful ensuing year. Improvement in all spheres stems from dissatisfaction with present conditions and I have never spoken to a coach who does not believe that he can do better next time by altering some part of his programme.

The business of creating an environment in which swimmers are involved in their training as well as in competition requires an individual with powers of leadership and a flair for ensuring that each swimmer has a task to perform which will be both satisfying to him and of value to the group as a whole.

Conditions are ever-changing and parts of the unit can break down, so he must have his finger constantly on the pulse of the club so as to eradicate problems at their very outset. This is a mammoth task, but one that is being handled successfully by numerous coaches throughout the world. Their personalities differ considerably yet they all have the ability to bring out the best in the individual and to deal with all the associated problems of maturity. An American coach was reported as saying that he uses plenty of a particular four-letter word in his programme – 'love'. He enjoys working with people, whereas some so-called coaches appear merely to put up with the swimmers and regard them as machines to be trained, not as people to be spoken to. What a short-sighted policy this is.

I have said nothing about the woman coach and the part she plays in the sport. All my examples have been directed towards men because I have met very few women coaching top swimmers. There are exceptions: Roland Mathes is coached by a woman and Ursula Carlile is responsible for a considerable amount of the success story of the Ryde Swimming Club in Australia. I have seen a number of women coaches attached to the Eastern European swimming teams, which may be a reflection of their type of society and the positive role women play in it, especially in the professions. There is no reason why women should not make successful coaches in Britain if they can command the respect of the swimmers by creating the conditions outlined in this chapter.

I am sure that many swimmers do not believe that coaches feel any emotion whatsoever; yet this could not be further removed from the truth. Feelings have to be controlled, especially before important races when a swimmer is in a highly emotional state and could easily be affected by the feelings of the coach. If he shows that he is as anxious as the swimmer then the swimmer may feel that he does not have much faith in his ability to achieve the specified objective. On the exterior the coach is a picture of confidence and serenity, while his heart is blowing a gasket. A coach has a right to be nervous when he considers that it is only in competition that he can really measure the success or failure of his system. If things do go wrong it is very difficult to isolate the root causes from a programme which involves so many variables. 'Was the taper too long?' 'Did we do enough conditioning work?' 'Did they warm up properly?' The questions are unending, but whatever the reasons the pieces have to be picked up and the hard work must start once again. Courage is needed to experiment and find out what went wrong; the coach must not withdraw into his shell, lick his wounds and sulk. There is no place for negative thinking if energy is to be applied next time in the right place to achieve the desired results.

My tour of America brought me into close contact with the great names in the world of swimming coaching. Their success was the direct result of years of hard work to produce the right environment to develop the potentialities of their swimmers. Many of them had fought for more training facilities and were still not completely satisfied. The competition between them was very fierce and there was no place for the coach who wanted to dabble in competitive swimming. They were totally committed to producing powerful teams and nowhere did I find a coach who worked with just a few swimmers. Don Gambril of Long Beach State College, Los Angeles, firmly believed that he must put in far more work than his swimmers if he is to keep his organization in a position to respond to any unexpected changes.

Coaches come in all shapes and sizes and from a variety of social and academic backgrounds but they must all have the ability to work with young people. Because of the present turmoil in British swimming few British coaches have an opportunity to build powerful teams and gain experience in the craft of producing united team efforts from vast numbers of individuals. They therefore miss much of the fun and satisfaction that is part and parcel of team swimming and the fulfilment of the coach's ambitions, because their qualities of leadership are never extended when they are dealing with just a few individuals.

13 The Swimmer

Who is the individual who will be prepared to submit to the rigours of four hours' daily training for the sake of a race which may take less than a minute to complete? Does he derive satisfaction from taking part in a sport or is he using it as a vehicle to achieve success and establish himself among his peers? I certainly do not profess to know the answers to these questions, but it has been my experience that the real competitors have an insatiable thirst for winning. To some, second best is not good enough, whereas others have a lower level of ambition. In the last chapter we saw how the coach can have considerable effect on the individual's motivation and it may well be that many swimmers are spurred on to work hard because their objectives are in unison with those of the coach. One question I have put to many British swimmers is this: if they were able to choose the sport in which they would most like to be gifted what would it be? Most choose an activity like soccer or tennis where they could receive considerable kudos and a comfortable standard of living. They all felt that it must be marvellous to find somebody to pay you to work at an activity you enjoy doing; the other man's grass is always greener!

Whether or not swimmers find their swimming career a satisfactory interlude in their life is far more important than their motives for swimming. I remember once describing a swimmer of mine as a mixture of a masochist and a sadist, in as much as he could subject himself to no end of punishment in training yet in competition he showed not the slightest mercy for his opponents. Perhaps 'selfish' would be a more accurate assessment, because he was spurred on to intense training only because of his personal desire to overcome all opposition. I hasten to add that I do not use 'selfish' in a derogatory sense, but more as a way of describing internal motivation. The younger swimmer can be persuaded to train hard by his parents or his coach, but only for so long. Eventually he will mature sufficiently to reason out his own ideals and rationalize swimming with the many other aspects of his life, such as future career, social life and other sporting or intellectual activities. When this happens the coach must be prepared for the worst and accept that some swimmers will no longer place competitive swimming high on their list of priorities. What I am saying is that until a swimmer commits himself to the sport he will never have an opportunity to develop his talent. There are many swimmers who train daily but who are never fully committed to their work or swimming racing. Such individuals often go through the motions of training without too much mental involvement. We cannot expect this sort of reasoning from the younger age-group and for this reason their programme should be different from that of the older swimmer. An American university student once told me that he had become sickened by swimming because after fifteen years in the sport it no longer held his interest; he knew that he would never improve because the motivating force had left him. Skilful handling on the part of the coach can make a swimmer want to work and compete, but it cannot force the issue.

To rationalize the sport a swimmer will need to be pretty intelligent: the chances of a dull individual reaching the dizzy heights of swimming are becoming slimmer each year as vast numbers of swimmers of equal fitness and physical attributes are using tactical ploys to oust the champion from his pedestal. Unchained physical ability did not win Carl Robie his gold medal in the 200-metres butterfly at the Mexico Olympics; this young man had the intelligence to expend his energy in a way that would be most destructive to the opposition. It does not follow that all top swimmers should be members of Mensa, but the intelligent swimmer needs to apply his brain power to the business of successfully controlling his body to do the unexpected. Predictable swimmers are the easiest to beat unless, of course, they are of the calibre of Roland Mathes, whose overriding quality is that he always wins backcrawl races. American swimmers strike me as having considerable maturity, which has been developed through tough competition in which the champions have captured and defended their position by their tactical skill in using their physical attributes. If this ability to select the right tactics for a particular race is combined with the physical conditions mentioned in chapter 1 then the perfect swimmer begins to emerge. Rarely do we find all these traits in one person, but there are swimmers with only average physical ability who reach the top because they possess intelligence and a burning desire to be successful. The most frustrating swimmers for the coach to handle are those with intelligence and physical ability but no particular interest in reaching the top.

The reader may argue that physical and mental maturity are not essential qualities for a true champion. A champion may be seen as a swimmer holding a world record, but I prefer to see him as one who can win the races which matter. Mark Spitz was holder of the world record for 100- and 200-metres butterfly in 1968 yet failed to win a gold medal in these Olympic events; I wouldn't mind betting that he would have forfeited his world marks for just one gold medal, because a silver or bronze medal is only a consolation prize for having failed. My hero, Roland Mathes, is the epitomy of a champion because he holds gold medals *and* world records.

A FINA[12] medical team reporting in 1969 was gravely concerned at the problems resulting from champion swimmers becoming younger. I would agree that over the last twenty

L

years the sport has attracted youngsters in their thousands, but I would not agree that 'champions' are becoming any younger, for the reasons stated above. I do believe, however, that a valid reason for swimmers generally being younger than their predecessors of ten or twenty years ago is that the older person with a career and family to consider cannot afford the time to train unless the State is prepared to foot the bill, which is what happens in many East European countries. To take one example, Roy Saari, the American freestyler who attended the 1964 Olympics in Tokyo, seriously considered entering the trials for the 1968 Games. It was only when he considered the implications of selection and the prospect of attending a two-month training camp that he realized his folly, because with a wife and family and a job that relied on sales he could not possibly afford the time.

American male swimmers have an added incentive to stay in the sport until their early twenties because of the importance placed on swimming in their universities, though as an inter-college activity it ranks behind basketball and football. As these halls of learning believe that their image can be greatly enhanced by athletic as well as academic achievement they attempt to attract gifted performers to their fold. Each university has an athletics department responsible for the organization of inter-college sport. This has a budget that can be used by the coaches to attract athletes; they can offer to pay all or part of their tuition and subsistence if they satisfy the university authorities as to their academic prowess. Most ambitious swimmers strive to attract the attention of a university coach, especially one attached to one of the universities noted for their high academic and sporting standards. An education in a top university can be a very expensive affair and a sporting or academic scholarship may be a swimmer's passport to a bright future. (In Britain, there are no sporting scholarships as such but grants are far easier to come by.) The American swimmer who has been awarded a scholarship will be allowed to remain in the university only if he continually meets the requirements of both athletic and academic departments. Over his four-year course he adapts to these pressures and this is reflected in his athletic performance because he realizes that his whole future may depend on the way he reacts to his university work. Women's university swimming is not regarded as being as important as the male programme and consequently the same powerful athletic scholarship scheme does not exist. Peter Daland, coach of the University of Southern California team, told me that he did not believe that women's swimming would ever reach the same heights because after a year or two in university women tend to drift away from the sport as their involvement in other more social activities develops. Whatever the reason, the top American women swimmers generally retire at about eighteen, when swimming becomes just one of their many interests.

There has been much speculation on how the Eastern European countries attract and hold talent in swimming, with theories ranging from the cynics who believe that the threat of the salt-mine is enough to make anybody work hard, to the more liberal view, held by myself, that the talent is selected and placed in an establishment which can offer excellent training as well as a first-class education. East Germany's rapid rise to the ranks of a world sporting power is not the result of sadistic exploitation of talent but rather the implementation of a scheme that offers a gifted child an attractive life both in the immediate future and when his swimming career is ended. I well remember the East German men's medley team in the finals in Mexico: their spirit was second to none, whereas the Russian team appeared to be dejected and completely uninterested in the ensuing race. It struck me that the system adopted for training the Russian swimmers may have been as physiologically sound as their German neighbours, but they had neglected to consider the individual swimmer's sense of satisfaction. Before the Olympic 200-metres butterfly final I went with Martyn Woodroffe into the competitors' rest area and was chatting with him about his plans for the race when I suddenly noticed the two Russian boys who had also made the final. They were lying on camp beds staring into oblivion and looking very frightened. During the hour before the beginning of that race nobody came to talk to these two boys and this, to me, reflected the very clinical approach of the chief Russian coach. Needless to say, they did not win a medal and the Russian team as a whole was severely criticized for its poor showing. Much publicity has been given to American soldiers who have no interest in fighting the war in Vietnam, the point being that training and first-class equipment is of little use if the leaders cannot convince the soldiers that the battle is worth fighting. I believe that the same applies to swimming.

We have seen that age and type of experience can have considerable effect upon a swimmer's competitive performance. The early twenties is an ideal period for performance from male swimmers; this may also be true of women, but very few stay around long enough to give us any real proof. World records have been broken by twelve-year-olds; the South African backcrawler, Karen Muir, is a case in point but even she did faster times when she was sixteen. The better performance could be the result of many factors such as increased strength, longer levers, mental stability or a greater personal desire to win. The reasons are not as important as the knowledge that better performances do go hand in hand with all-round maturity, always provided that personal ambition is high.

14 Age-Group Swimming

In the last chapter I attempted to outline a few of the attributes of the successful swimmer, which include that of maturity. Yet throughout the world we are finding a rapid increase in age-group swimming. Competition exists for under-tens, under twelves, under-fourteens, under-sixteens, all of which would appear to be a contradiction to my plea for mature swimmers. The original aim of the age-group programme was to encourage youngsters to take part in the sport against opposition of similar ages and physical build rather than to throw them in at the deep end against swimmers who were much older and superior. Age is certainly not the best way to match competitors because of the different rates at which youngsters mature. One has only to look at a town's under-fifteen soccer team to see that it contains young men, not a group of little sopranos. The early developer has more chance of making a team than his late-developing classmates because he is taller, stronger and faster and can use his brain more effectively. Experiments have been carried out in many countries in an attempt to develop an age-group structure based on developmental rather than chronological ages. All, so far, have proved impractical because the business of testing and measuring each child is too time-consuming. Yet we must accept that age-group swimming is here to stay and endeavour to overcome these obstacles.

The broad base of swimming is the age-group programme and the involvement of such young children automatically means that parents will play a very important part. This may take the form of running the youngsters to and from practices or even that of acting as coach. The latter can have very serious consequences when a family begins to eat, sleep and breathe swimming. How difficult it must be in this situation to understand that swimming is only one of many interests that the youngster would like to pursue. I have known numerous cases where the child enjoys training but hates competition and it is my belief that too much pressure applied at this time by parents or coach can have disastrous consequences. They may take the form of a complete rebellion against the sport and all those people connected with it, including parents, or of the more subtle tactics of feigning illness during work-outs or competition. The old saying, 'We can lead a horse to water but we cannot make him drink', applies to age-groupers as well as to the older swimmer.

Larry Raymond[13] places all the blame for the problems facing American age-group swimming on the shoulders of the age-group coaches, highlighting their general unwillingness to educate parents. I am sure that numerous coaches could quote cases of parents admonishing their children for losing races which they considered to be a 'walkover'. Perhaps it would be a good thing if some of these parents stopped continuing the war of words at home. Knowing my personal make-up as I do, I am sure that I would have reacted very strongly to parents interfering in my physical recreation. After all, I was the one who took up the activity and trained every day and if I messed a race up then I would already be upset without other people making matters worse.

At the risk of becoming yet another 'agony column' expert I feel that I should offer some advice to parents whose children are involved in age-group swimming. Always bear in mind that the aim of the programme is to introduce children to the competitive side of swimming in such a way that they will find racing attractive and will be motivated to train. Love and security are considered by child-guidance experts to be the essentials for the happy development of children; studies of thousands of delinquents point to a lack of these two essentials in their lives causing them to behave in a neurotic manner. This insecurity is expressed in the feeling of deprivation of love. The younger the child, the more love and protection he requires from both parents. Please don't think that I would like to protect the child from all exterior pressures, but I should like to see a home environment where the child can retreat when the going becomes too rough, a place where he knows he can rest and receive encouragement from his parents. He needs this because the pressures of swimming and training on a youngster are considerable. I remember that in my own childhood I thought that there could be nothing worse on God's earth than examinations. The situation was always made worse because I knew that I would never do very well in them, thus exposing myself to a showdown at home. As an adult I find that the pressures of running a mortgage, a car and so on are nowhere near as upsetting as the examination period of childhood. It is very difficult for an adult to appreciate fully the working of a child's mind and too few parents of young swimmers have been competitors in the sport themselves so that it becomes easy for them to criticize the actions of others.

The worst feeling in any race is to be ahead and then to find another person challenging and beginning to overtake. Obviously a counter challenge will be made, but if this does not come off all the previous training in the world will have little effect on the final result: the right challenge at the right moment can break the swimmer's psychological prowess. Youngsters cannot generally cope with these variables in the same way as their older brothers and sisters and parents and coaches must accept this fact. Even if a ten-year-old is always winning, his performance should be put into perspective: a 75-second 100-metre freestyle swim may rate number one in his age group, but he may well be the two hundredth fastest freestyler of junior or senior ranking. It takes very responsible parents not to go over the moon when their youngster becomes an age-group champion, but how disillusioned they will become when their ten-year-old champion is dethroned at twelve! Lack of training or competitive attitude may have nothing to do with the defeat; another youngster may have matured at a faster rate and be just too big and strong. Gary Hall, the world 400-metres individual medley record holder, smashed all American records of his age group when he was ten years old and then went into the wilderness until he was sixteen. He was saved from utter oblivion by a coach and parents who had faith in his ability and sufficient commonsense not to knock him when he was down. Countries with the population of Britain and Australia cannot afford to have swimming drop-outs amongst the younger element.

Parents can help their child by providing a secure home which offers good food, adequate sleep, and help with pro-gramming the day to fit in homework, training and other activities. A home where the child is encouraged, not forced to swim will go a long way to producing a real swimmer in the late teens. One mother whom I knew very well told her young son that he loved swimming and would force him to train and compete. She wanted so much to see her son succeed that her personal ambition was beginning to conflict with her love for her son. Needless to say, the young lad replaced swimming with other activities as soon as he was able to stand up for himself. It is folly to fête the age-group champion, especially if his success has been achieved by a physique which is superior to the other youngsters'. The ideal parent, then, will take a keen interest in the child's swimming but will realize the serious consequences of interfering and curtailing his freedom to involve himself on his own terms.

'Age-group swimming would be a damned sight better without parents' – I have heard this type of quote from coaches far too many times. Parents produce, feed and clothe the age-grouper and it would be ridiculous completely to exclude them from playing a useful part in the swimming programme. We have seen the part that a parent can play but if this is done properly they should expect the coach to play an equally responsible role. Before embarking upon any programme a coach should have a philosophy of coaching to which he is going to adhere. I feel that his age-group philosophy should include an all-round development of the youngsters by placing them in a swimming situation which they find sufficiently satisfying to encourage them to respond in a positive way to their surroundings. Like the parents, he cannot force the youngsters to train harder. Once he has a philosophy he should go out of his way to educate parents as to his aims and methods of obtaining them. A parent who does not agree can cause much ill-feeling in a club unless he is isolated and given an ultimatum: he must either accept the thinking or move to some other outfit. There will always be differences of opinion and the strong coach should have a meeting with parents and swimmers to iron out the problems quickly and smoothly. Every coach can quote cases of certain parents undermining the coach-swimmer relationship by expressing their disagreement with the coach's methods. This is just one way of making a child insecure which could have damaging effects in activities other than swimming. Parents may resent the tremendous influence the coach has over their children but if they want to see success they must accept that their children's life will not always revolve round them.

A conscientious age-group coach may be genuinely frightened by the problems of marrying swimming with the growth and development of the swimmers without creating a situation which is detrimental to either. Coaches who do not admit that these problems exist destroy talent before it has a chance to be nurtured. The age-group dilemma is made much easier if coaches are responsible for running a full club programme that includes the senior squad. In such a case the coach will use his age-group swimming to attract and maintain the interest of youngsters, in the hope that he can hold them until they are in their late teens. Some of these swimmers may be prominent age-groupers throughout their career, but the coach will not allow the success to accelerate his development programme so much that it may have detrimental effects later on. The best analogy concerning when to work age-group swimmers was made by a New Zealand swimming coach at the 1970 Commonwealth Games. He likened the development of swimmers to fruit ripening on a tree: 'Some ripens before others and you pick it. It's no use picking it before it's ripe or when it's over-ripe.' From this analogy we can see that a universal rule of training cannot be applied, but the coach can provide the incentives for training and competition. If the response is there the pressures can be increased, but the coach must always be alert to the effects of the pressure on the youngsters.

Every fallen age-grouper represents years of hard work wasted for ever. We cannot afford the tremendous wastage caused by age-group swimming becoming an end in itself rather than a means to an end. Some may say that the programme in Britain it not failing, but there is certainly no evidence to suggest that age-group swimming is raising the standard of Britain's international team. The type of competition must be questioned, for it may be that relatively short 100- and 200-metre races do not have any carry-over to the 400- and 1500-metre swims that some British swimmers will experience when they enter senior competition. The uninformed often say that there is reason why youngsters should not train over longer distances even though competition is not provided. Yet what motivation will a youngster have to train over these distances if he cannot compete over them as well? British distance swimmers are completely naïve when it comes to competing because there is not enough opportunity or incentive in internal competition.

British swimming has a very broad base in its age-group programme but does not possess a system that is capable of developing the full potential of all this talent. The system depends on the ability of coach, administrator and parent to accept, first of all, that age-group swimming is an introduction and then to decide what form the introduction should take. To date, the system has been able to identify talent but has failed miserably in developing and perfecting it.

Epilogue

Swimming training is becoming more technical and coaches are being bombarded with new information almost every day. Much of this information has to be converted into practical use by the coach, who relies upon his ability to communicate with his swimmers in such a way that they are prepared to accept his advice. It is up to him to create the swimming environment that will encourage the swimmers to train and compete effectively. There are swimmers in the world who are training four hours per day but British coaches cannot ask their swimmers to do likewise if they do not have a carrot to dangle in front of them.

There has been very little change in stroke technique over the last five years or, for that matter, in the physiology of exercise, yet world times are still improving. The kudos attached to success is obviously encouraging certain countries and groups of swimmers to put more effort into their daily training. America and the Eastern European countries have slotted swimming and other sports into their educational system, but the prospect of a similar situation being created in Britain seems very slim, since her educationists and amateur sporting purists seem to object to a system being created that could challenge the rest of the world. As they call the tune coaches can do very little about it at present. Britain loves a winner but is not convinced of the value of intense sport in creating more winners.

Because little importance is attached to athletic prowess in Britain, swimming is not attracting sufficient coaches who are capable of continuous dialogue with young people. How many British coaches really try to understand their swimmers and really involve them in their training programme? We cannot have the blind leading the blind. The British Government and other governing bodies merely pay lip-service to the pleas of coaches for change, but this may be because we coaches do not present our case well.

I trust that the reader will see from this book that there is far more to swimming coaching than meets the eye. Many of the ideas expressed are my own and, so far, have brought success. In the future they will probably be of little use as techniques become more objective. I hope that they will assist many of you to start your careers in competitive swimming, but please don't take everything for granted. If the reader begins to question my ideas then the book has achieved its aim of encouraging him to question the ideas of others and his own.

Notes

1 Charles Newman, *Horlicks Textbook of Land Swimming Drill with Music*, 1915.
2 Forbes Carlile, *Swimming*, Pelham Books, 1963.
3 James E. Councilman, *The Science of Swimming*, Pelham Books, 1968.
4 K. Lovell, *Educational Psychology and Children*, University of London Press, 1969.
5 B. R. Pugelski, *Psychology of Learning*, Holt, Rinehart & Winston, New York, 1956.
6 Leo Hendry, *Coaches Bulletin* No. 46 (BSCA).
7 C. W. Thompson, *Manual of Structural Kinesiology*, C. B. Mosby, St Louis, 1969.
8 England has no club championship events in its short-course championship programme.
9 Harry Braund, *The Role of the Coach*, BSCA Annual Conference 1971.
10 Lord Montgomery, *Forward from Victory*, Hutchinson, 1948.
11 Sir Roger Falk, *Business of Management*, Penguin, 1970.
12 *Federation Internationale de Natation Amateur*, International Governing Body of Swimming.
13 Larry Raymond: Chairman, Age Group Coaches, American Swimming Coaches Association, Coach of Woodland Hills Swim Club, California.

Select Bibliography

Coaches Bulletin, British Swimming Coaches Association.
Hadfield, J. A., *Childhood and Adolescence*, Penguin, 1962.
Karpovitch, *Physiology of Muscular Activity*, W. B. Saunders 1965.
Knapp, B., *Skill in Sport*, Routledge & Kegan Paul, 1963.